# Hurricane Hilary

## The Ultimate Hurricane Survival Guide

*(Your Emergency Essentials Guide for Hurricane Preparedness)*

**Daryl Mackey**

Published By **Tyson Maxwell**

**Daryl Mackey**

All Rights Reserved

*Hurricane Hilary: The Ultimate Hurricane Survival Guide (Your Emergency Essentials Guide for Hurricane Preparedness)*

**ISBN 978-0-9958936-4-1**

No part of this guidebook shall be reproduced in any form without permission in writing from the publisher except in the case of brief quotations embodied in critical articles or reviews.

Legal & Disclaimer

The information contained in this book is not designed to replace or take the place of any form of medicine or professional medical advice. The information in this book has been provided for educational & entertainment purposes only.

The information contained in this book has been compiled from sources deemed reliable, and it is accurate to the best of the Author's knowledge; however, the Author cannot guarantee its accuracy and validity and cannot be held liable for any errors or omissions. Changes are periodically made to this book. You must consult your doctor or get professional medical advice before using any of the suggested remedies, techniques, or information in this book.

Upon using the information contained in this book, you agree to hold harmless the Author from and against any damages, costs, and expenses, including any legal fees potentially resulting from the application of any of the information provided by this guide. This disclaimer applies to any damages or injury caused by the use and application, whether directly or indirectly, of any advice or information presented, whether for breach of contract, tort, negligence, personal injury, criminal intent, or under any other cause of action.

You agree to accept all risks of using the information presented inside this book. You need to consult a professional medical practitioner in order to ensure you are both able and healthy enough to participate in this program.

Table Of Contents

Chapter 1: Understanding A Hurricane .... 1

Chapter 2: Everything To Do Before ......... 9

Chapter 3: Handbook For Surviving A Flood ............................................................. 25

Chapter 4: Facts And Myths About Hurricanes ............................................. 33

Chapter 5: Hurricane Preparedness Manual For Businesses ........................... 38

Chapter 6: 11 Things You Must Never Do In The Event Of A Hurricane ....................... 49

Chapter 7: 21 Smart Steps That You Can Make ..................................................... 57

Chapter 8: A Dictionary Of Hurricane Terms .................................................... 75

Chapter 9: Attitudes ............................... 89

Chapter 10: Evacuation Or Travel ........ 108

Chapter 11: Basic Storm Safety ............ 123

Chapter 12: Analysis ........................... 144

Chapter 13: 1992 Hurricane Andrew .... 153

Chapter 14: Safety & Survival............... 165

Chapter 15: Understanding The Formation And Basics Of Hurricanes ..................... 175

**Chapter 1: Understanding A Hurricane**

A hurricane is one type of tropical cyclone which is able to traverse the entire length of the east coast and its coastline regions and barrier islands, bringing the rain to a torrent as well as strong winds, storm surges and floods up to two weeks in open oceans. It is the National Hurricane Center states that winds that reach speeds of be at or above 74 mph and are the only thing that defines an actual hurricane (anything lesser than that, and it is considered an tropical storm).

What distinguishes Hurricanes from tornadoes?

Although tornadoes typically form on the earth and are seldom bigger than a quarter-mile they are typically formed overseas, and are often several hundred miles in size. The duration of a hurricane can be months, however it could only last for a couple of minutes.

In its lifetime it is possible for a storm to be strengthened and then weaken several times. The hurricanes of the Atlantic Basin can begin as tropical storms or depressions, before getting stronger to the point of a particular classification according to the Saffir-Simpson Hurricane Wind Scale.

Most hurricanes attain their greatest strength just before they hit the ground. Once they're above the land, they quickly decrease their power since they are pushed by humid, warm atmospheric conditions over ocean water. It's possible for a storm to reach land once and make a return trip to the ocean grow stronger, and possibly come back to land in the next or third time.

To illustrate as an example, As an example, Hurricane Isbell that formed within the Caribbean in 1964, initially arrived at the western coast of Cuba. It was a Category 2 hurricane the storm continued its move to the northeast, and finally made its way to Everglade City in Florida. The storm crossed into the state but then weakened and went away close to West Palm Beach When it crossed the Atlantic Ocean to the north then turning west. It returned to shore near Morehead City, North Carolina.

The following year the following year, hurricane Betsy arrived in Key Largo after moving west from the Atlantic. The storm swiftly entered into the Gulf of Mexico from the west, then turned to the towards the north, gaining strength to transform into an Category 4 storm and then made landfall near New Orleans. When the remnants of the storm travelled across the country and rained down on Mississippi, Arkansas, Ohio as well as Pennsylvania.

In 2004 the 2004 hurricane Jeanne hit Puerto Rico before heading north to the Atlantic before heading westward to Florida. The hurricane had spent an extensive period of time in Florida and the Atlantic, the hurricane made an appearance in the same place that the Hurricane Frances was just a couple of days earlier.

The hurricane Jeanne diminished as it moved through Georgia, South Carolina, North Carolina, and Virginia before it returned in its home in the Atlantic via Washington, D.C. Hurricane Jeanne was initially an tropical storm and later it became a depression.

However the tornadoes are purely natural phenomena that occur in the region. The longest tornado known path was recorded to originate from Missouri in 1925, and finished after an eastward trip towards Indiana. It killed 695 people, but that tornado was also among the deadliest.

Understanding the development of tornadoes and hurricanes

The supercell storms are mesocyclones which effectively rotate the winds of thousands of miles in the air. They produce rain that makes air descend into the form of a "back flank downdraft," that causes mesocyclone's wind to fall. The mesocyclone pulls moist air from the lower downdraft to the cloud's base. There, it blends it with the warm air of an updraft. This creates the cloud wall that spins.

At first, storms can also bring humid and warm atmospheric air from the surface of the ocean to the upper atmosphere. The warm ocean air flows towards the sky, then cools, and eventually condenses into small water droplets which release energy which fuels the storm. Once the droplets of water are returned to ground to complete the process the convective cells begin to form. They are formed when the Coriolis influence causes the wind caused by temperature and pressure variations to spin.

The tornadoes and hurricanes are shaped similarly however, hurricanes possess an even larger source of fuel that is humid, warm air that is soaring over the surface of the ocean.

Can Hurricanes Create Tornadoes?

In reality, tornadoes can be created by hurricanes on the land. In the event that a tropical storm hits land and there is plenty of the thunderclouds which are crucial for the creation of tornadoes. The typical scenario is

Hurricanes can cause swift shifts in speed and direction.

Twirling rolls of air, caused by the force of winds shear create vortices.

Tornadoes are possible in thunderstorms when updrafts from vortices and storms are in contact.

The atmospheric effects of hurricanes already encourage the formation of tornadoes. They are almost guaranteed once the impacts of the hurricane's wind shear are considered.

If you do not live in the vicinity of the coastline however, tornadoes may still cause destruction to your property regardless of whether it's within the predicted direct direction. Be aware of local warnings for tornadoes as storm-generated tornadoes could occur up to several hundred kilometers from where the storm made landfall.

An incoming hurricane or tornado may result in wind damages to your property therefore you must verify the insurance coverage of your home to ensure that you're protected. In the event of a hurricane striking Florida insurers get flooded with demands. Claim adjusters overworked tend to make mistakes and, in most cases, are driven to reject or underestimate claims.

If the insurer has refused to pay for a wind-related claim that is valid then you may need to look into an attorney for property damage.

**Chapter 2: Everything To Do Before**

What do you do if there is a chance of a storm? Do not be worried. We have compiled a checklist of things to consider before, during, and following a hurricane. It is vital to be prepared if you reside in an area that is vulnerable. The possibility of tropical or hurricane-forced storms is that they could impact any region or region of United States' Gulf Coast or Atlantic Seaboard.

With the help of experts from the National Hurricane Center, FEMA as well as FEMA, and the American Red Cross, the below checklist was developed.

Guidelines for Hurricane Safety

Before A Hurricane

Secure your property. In the case of doors and windows most effective protection is offered through permanent storm shutters. Another option is to put up a cover your windows with five-inch" marine plywood which has been cut into the proper size and prepared to install Glass that crashes through windows cannot be prevented by the use of tape.

To ensure that you can securely attach your roof to the frame and install the straps or clips the straps will help prevent damage to your roof.

Reduce the chance of falling branches and other debris by trimming surrounding trees and shrubs Residence.

To stop floods that aren't meant to be to occur, clear your gutters and downspouts from all dirt.

Choose the best location and method to secure your boat if you are the owner of one.

Keep things in your basement so that you can prevent flooding, even a minor one, from damaging the items.

The items you value should be secured placed on the upper floor in your home. Photograph albums and other souvenirs are included in this group.

Chemicals used in the home should be stocked on high shelves fitted with lids that are tight. In the event that chemicals are mixed with floodwaters, they can be extremely dangerous and harmful.

You can think about building the safest room.

Invest in the purchase of a fire extinguisher.

Make sure that your pet's ID is tagged.

Create a folder of the necessary documents to carry along in the event that you require them to get insurance at some point in the future! Photograph important documents like passports, prescriptions and tax returns as well as social security cards, driver's licenses and other documents that are legal. To save the photos and upload them to the internet, you can do so Store physical copies in a bag with a watertight.

If you are ever without power, be sure to have an emergency kit. Included in the kit are prescribed medications, as well as three days worth of water, food and cash (along with any pets).

Check out all shelters within your neighborhood. Keep an eye on your escape route. If you need to, keep bags ready "to go."

Fill plastic bottles up with water to drink. Think about what you'd need in the event that you were to be stuck for a prolonged period and had to face the possibility of a power failure.

Make sure you fill up the tank of your car.

Download the Red Cross Emergency App on your Android or iPhone. Send the text "GETCANE" to 90999 instead.

As A Hurricane Approaches

*If a storm is predicted to hit land close to you, it is recommended that you

Keep track of the weather on local radio stations, NOAA TV, radio and on the web to stay updated. Make sure you are aware of any evacuation alerts.

Make sure to close the storm shutters, and then secure the home. The force of strong winds can be used to carry up and smash even awnings. They can then turn into projectsiles.

Take inside or secure the outside furniture, grills bikes, garbage bins as well as hanging plants, tools, and garden equipment.

If authorities tell you to shut off your appliances. If not, adjust the temperature of the refrigerator and freezer at the lowest setting and then keep your doors closed.

Remove freezer-friendly items from the fridge.

OPT-OFFSET your propane tank.

The devices that are used should be moved to shelves that are higher in order to avoid water harm.

The cell phone must be fully charged and ready to be used. Then, you should not use it, unless you are in a genuine need to use it in an emergency.

Be aware that you should have a specific amount of cash in your account. Power outages could stop ATMs from working.

If you're able to find enough time, you can moor your vessel.

It is important to ensure that there is enough water for hygiene purposes such as toilet flushing and cleaning. It is recommended to add water into the bathtub as well as similar containers.

*Prescription medicines including a fire extinguisher a first-aid kit, an emergency flashlight with batteries bedding and sleeping bags cooking and eating equipment cans, food items and bottle of water, jumper cables the paper map, a toilet roll as well as personal items for care as well as rain gear, should be kept with you always.

Keep within.

When To Evacuate:

If you're directed to do this by the city's officials. Take their advice and do the procedure immediately (do not put off! ).

A mobile home or similar temporary structure is very risky during storms (no matter how secure onto the earth).

The strength of hurricane winds is greater in higher altitudes, so take care if you live in an apartment building that is high-rise.

If your residence is near to an inland waterway, river or floodplain. shoreline.

If you feel that your security is in danger.

If you're separated from your family members, plan a place to meet! Uncertainty about whether your family members are protected during a natural disaster is one of the main challenges. Remember that there are times when cellphones won't work. Communication is essential similar to the "old" days.

After authorities have declared safe, return. Avoid entering any waterways that are flooded! Avoid traveling on roads with flooding either by foot or car.

During Impact- While The Hurricane Still Rages

*

Go to your secure area if you've not yet done it. If you do not have any safe place, be sure to adhere to these guidelines:

Beware of all windows, skylights and glass doors. Stay within. Find a safe place like the closet, an interior room or a bathroom in the basement.

Lock and brace the doors that are exterior while locking all doors within.

Keep your curtains and blinds shut. If you notice a calm, do not get deceived. It could be the eye of the storm, and winds could get stronger.

On the lower level you can seek shelter in an interior room, closet or a hallway.

If you are lying on a table or another substantial object place it on the ground.

You can listen to the most important warnings about the weather, storm information as well as instructions via an audio portable radio.

Don't leave the safety of your residence or place of refuge before you know that the storm has passed towards. Although severe winds may be in the forecast, the eye of the storm could provide a short and unintentional break.

Make sure to keep your refrigerator shut in the event of power failure to ensure that cold air stays inside and to prevent food items that are perishable from getting spoiled.

Make use of a portable generator strictly as recommended by the manufacturer. To prevent electric shock, generators must be grounded in a safe manner. Generators should never be installed indoors in garages or basements. They should also not be used in locations where doors, windows or vents are located close to. Given that generators release CO. (CO) ensure that your house is fitted with a CO detector that is functional.

Following A Hurricane

If you're evacuated, do not return until you have been told by the authorities that it's okay to.

Beware of the possibility of falling power lines. Avoid touching objects that come in contact with electrical lines, particularly any waters or puddles of water that might be in close proximity to fallen power lines.

If you can board up windows with damage You can stop vandalism as well as further harm to your property. Consider a fix that is affordable and temporary.

Take care of any gas lines which the storm might have damaged or destroyed. If gas leaks are suspect, wait until the company that provides the service determines it safe to access the premises.

Be aware of the dangers associated with storms like water caused by floods, sharp or damaged objects, tree branches that are broken or other structures due to strong winds or floods.

Make detailed financial records, retain all invoices as well as receipts for interim repairs. (Refrain from completing permanent repairs until after your Claim specialist has evaluated the issue.) Make sure you keep a thorough record of all other expenses.

Take inventory of any personal property damaged and then separate it. Create a list of items damaged, listing every item's description, its brand and age, as well as the manufacturer's name as well as, if available where it was purchased and the date of the purchase. Include any photos, videos or inventory of your belongings that you might already possess.

Contact your insurance company about finding temporary accommodations in the event that you think your house could be a risk due to the storm.

Recovering from the effects of a catastrophe typically is a lengthy process. It is the most important thing to consider security, along with physical and mental wellbeing.

Tell your family and friends they are secure.

To stay safe from electrical hazards as well as other hazards Do not leave home in the absence of permission.

If you're not given the permission to drink tap water.

Check the refrigerator or freezer's temperature. It is safe to eat food that is kept at 40 degrees Fahrenheit or less. If not, you should throw it out for safety reasons.

Dispose of any food item which has come in contact with the floodwaters and also, since it could contain chemical compounds or waterborne disease, etc. Better to be safe instead of being sorry.

Get in touch with your insurance company and get photos of the damage.

Damaged items from water should be taken out of your house immediately or sold. This is essential in order to minimize the likelihood of mold growing inside your home.

Avoid walking or driving through floodwaters that could be electrically affected or polluted; even 6 inches of water rushing can send a man to the floor. Don't underestimate the power of water moving.

Things To Take Note Of Before Returning To Your Home/ Property Following A Hurricane

It is essential to take the time to contemplate your needs prior to heading back home to your residence or work place following an event such as a hurricane or a tornado, even if you had to leave or opted to do so.

You should only return to your place of residence or of employment only when the authorities have given permission to return. If you tune into the TV, radio and other social media channels to stay informed on any change in climate or other weather conditions and also any directions issued by the authorities. Potentially dangerous situations, like damaged power lines or wires as well as gas leaks, flooding zones, trees damaged, as well as other debris, might be caused by the storm. Once you return to your home or workplace take care to be aware.

## Chapter 3: Handbook For Surviving A Flood

In the case of the storms and hurricanes, flooding typically have more damaging effect than winds. Are you located in an area that is prone to flooding? The most frequently occurring natural catastrophe within the United States is flooding, that is usually caused by sudden and intense rainfall. Check out these flood safety tips immediately for tips regarding how to be safe prior to, during and following a flood, for a better chance of survival as well as protect your belongings.

Flooding is the one hurricane/thunderstorm threat that results in the most fatalities annually. Flooding has been a cause of nearly 75% of declared disasters by the president.

The rainwater that is absorbed quicker than the soil or river are able to absorb is the primary reason behind flooding. It could be because of:

A stream or river which is overflowing into the adjacent region because of prolonged rain which lasts several days, intense rain lasting for only a brief duration, or debris or the formation of ice jams.

It can happen due to a levee controllable structure for water, such as dams, fail.

Plains, valleys floodplains, swamplands, coastlines, as well as anyplace in close proximity to large lakes are just a few of those areas that are susceptible to flooding.

Did you know: Flooding instead of high winds is what make hurricanes the strongest storms on Earth and one of the most destructive. Furthermore, if the zone is already flooding because of a hurricane it increases the chance that it will flood, potentially hundreds of miles in the inland!

Guidelines To Follow Before Floods

Be prepared! It's always a good idea prepare for any eventuality when you reside in a place that's vulnerable to flooding -- or even if there's no flooding in your area.

To get official flood updates be sure to pay focus on the TV, radio or on your cell phone. Know the difference between"watch" and "warning" "watch" and "warning":

If your area is in an emergency flood watch, then flooding may happen.

If you are under an alert for flooding, it means that the flood may be happening now or could happen very soon. Be prepared to go home immediately.

1 gallon of water per day per person not-perishable foods, a flashlight and a battery-powered or hand crank radio, a cellphone charger that is portable or solar additional batteries as well as a kit for first aid with a supply of 7 days worth of medicines as well as a multi-purpose tool items for personal hygiene and sanitation along with copies of vital personal papers should be stored in an emergency kit which will always be available.

Check that your drainage drainage channels and ditches don't get overflowing with rubbish This could cause flooding and the destruction of property.

Rapid flooding: Identify the potential for flash flooding. Make immediate moves towards higher ground if you think the flash flood could occur. Be sure to not wait for instructions prior to you move. Because of the power and the volume of water flash flooding is the single most fatal form of flooding.

Be on the lookout for streams, canals for drainage, canyons and many other locations susceptible to sudden flooding. In spite of the conventional warning signs, like rainfall clouds or heavy rain flash floods may occur in specific areas.

Guidelines To Follow During Floods

If necessary, evacuate

Evacuate the area if a flooding warning has been issued in your area. Transfer to a safer area and stay there until you are directed to evacuate the region.

Secure your home, when you can before the evacuation. Bring outdoor furnishings inside. Put your possessions that are most valuable in the uppermost point of the home's top floor.

If you are instructed to do this, turn off all utilities using main switches or valves. Disconnect all electrical equipment. If you're wet or sitting in water, do not touch the electrical devices.

Don't walk across a flowing body of water. The water could be carried away from your feet by 6 inches of flowing water. If you have to walk in the water, make sure you do it in areas where the current isn't. Verify the stability of the terrain in front using the help of a stick.

Don't drown, turn around! Turn around, stop, and take a different path when you come across a stream with water greater than the ankles of your feet. The strength and force of water is often underestimated.

Make sure that children are kept away from waters.

*Guidelines For Driving Through A Flood*

Things to consider prior:

If a vehicle is driving into flooding waters, nearly the drownings that result from flooding typically occur.

Take a different route another route in case you are faced with a road inundated.

Beware of driving through flood-prone regions. If the flood waters begin to inundate your car, it is best to take it off the road, and in the event that it's safe move to a higher level. The car could soon be removed along with your vehicle.

Many passenger cars are prone to losing control and could stop when 6 inches of water reaches their lowest point.

A large number of vehicles can float within a inch of water.

The majority of cars, including pickup trucks and SUVs are swept off by water that flows up to two feet in depth.

Guidelines To Follow After a Flood

If you're interested in knowing whether the water source of your community is safe for consumption take note of the media reports.

Do not swim in the floodwaters because they may contain either oil, sewage or both. Furthermore, electric lines underground or are buried may charge water.

Avoid the water that is moving.

Take note of the areas in which the flooding waters have receded. The weight of your vehicle can cause roads to degrade and fall.

Avoid touching downed electrical wires and report them to your company that provides the service.

## Chapter 4: Facts And Myths About Hurricanes

Get the most up-to-date information and statistics about hurricanes. How often do they happen? What are their locations? How harmful are they? What are you looking for in case a storm is on the approach, and what should you do in the event that something catastrophic happens? Learn the steps you need to take to make sure you are prepared for hurricanes.

The most costly and devastating natural disasters to have happened have been hurricanes. In order to protect your home and to keep you and your family members protected and safe It is crucial to plan your home and your family prior to a storm arrives and also to be aware of what you should do after the storm is over.

It's not difficult to fall for commonly held beliefs when trying to shield your family and possessions from Hurricane. If you're in a hurricane such as this it is possible that you have thought that sticking a huge "X" on your windows to prevent the windows from breaking and also ensure your safety. However, this "X" won't do anything to keep the wind from flying debris from breaking the glass. Installing storm shutters permanently or boarding your windows using marine plywood specially sized for the windows is an alternative.

One of the numerous misconceptions surrounding hurricane preparedness includes one of them being the "X" tape myth. Check out a few other popular myths concerning storms:

Myth #1: You only Have to Guard windows that face the water Windows that face the water storms could turn exterior objects such as landscaping materials into projectiles which could damage windows from any part of your home. To safeguard against powerful wind and flying objects the windows as well as glass doors need to be secure.

Myth 2: It is possible to stop the wind from blowing outward by leaning against the glass or a door.

If you are standing on the side of windows or doors, you put yourself in risk. It is better to stay away from windows and doors.

Beware of windows and doors made of glass.

In the event of a storm, you must lock the doors to your home and reinforce all exterior doors.

You can find a tiny internal space such as a closet or hallway located on the ground floor. you could make yourself at home.

Myth #4: Opening the windows will lessen stress

The myth of this urban legend rests by the notion that in an event of extreme weather, pressure could accumulate inside your house to the point that it collapses completely structurally. There is no way to make your home with airtightness, so the idea of overpressurizing at this level is not possible, as per the National Oceanic & Atmospheric Administration. The chance that flying objects enter your home increases as windows are open. So, in the event of a hurricane the windows should be secured by shutters.

Myth #4.

The most common misconception is that "It just cant" according to large portions in the United States, including both in the interior and on the coast often are subject to tropical storms as well as hurricanes' intense storm surges, floods and storm surges along the coast. Everyone hopes that they aren't impacted by a storm, however preparedness will make it better for you, your family and company.

## Chapter 5: Hurricane Preparedness Manual For Businesses

Don't wait until National Weather Service issues a warning about a hurricane to prepare when your company is located in an area that is susceptible to hurricanes. A few weeks or even months could be required to prepare and execute the actions which can safeguard your business and minimize the impact of a catastrophe.

Review your organization's preparations in case of a hurricane prior to hurricane season. After that, while you are able to make the preparations, create plans for protecting your business. These are a few steps you can take to guarantee your personnel's safety and your company during a natural disaster.

Planning Long-Term

Here are a few examples of long-term planning that can be carried out to improve the home's or company's general "hurricane readiness":

Examining the supports, guy wires as well as other components placed on roofs, to ensure that they're secure and in good working order.

Doors, windows, hinges and latches that are damaged or weak should be replaced or repaired.

Installing the mechanism for securing the windows and entrances to buildings (shutters and plywood. ).

Backup energy sources like generators. Testing this equipment on a regular basis.

Take steps to protect your home from water damage, if you reside in a flood zone.

If possible, construct levees or flood walls.

Sandbag placement must be considered if you are looking to prevent water from the construction.

Protect low-lying openings to buildings as well as entrances.

Do not store essential company equipment or supplies in the basement.

To stop reverse flow, put in shut-off valves in sewers and drainage lines.

Items in stock that could be damaged due to water damage on pallets or on racks.

Provide the pump house to flood-proof the fire sprinklers.

Secure central location should be selected to set up an emergency response group and take all necessary equipment and supplies. equipment. Every year prior to the start of hurricane season check these equipment and supplies. Some examples of equipment and other supplies that you should have in your arsenal are:

Pumps, hoses and mobiles

Mops and squeezers

Emergency illumination

Sandbags, sand and Sand

The shovel and axe

Sheets of plastic or tarpaulin

Nails and wood

Power and manual tools, as well as power tools.

Schematics for building and construction

Ropes/fasteners

Make a note of the outdoors tools and other equipment which will require to be kept safe. These could contain gas cylinders, liquid flammable barrels, tanks for propane and various other potentially hazardous substances.

Find a safe place to keep mobile equipment and vehicles prior to their arrival. This will ensure they are protected from abrasions caused by rain and fierce storms.

Make arrangements with suppliers to restore essential equipment and machinery in addition to the maintenance of buildings and other materials.

Short-Term Preparedness For Planning Ahead Of An Approaching Hurricane

Future plans are best made ahead of the possibility of a storm. In contrast to planning for the long term, it's best to implement these strategies in action before a storm or another severe weather event is forecast. Be aware of these points when you are getting set for business:

To help you determine the best time to take steps, you must closely follow forecasts for the weather.

Make sure that the information is accurate in your contact details for employees.

To protect the structure from debris flying around Secure the doors and windows as well as shuttering or boarding to seal any cracks.

The drainage pump are to be looked at, along with catch basins.

Transport mobile devices as well as vehicles to a secured zone.

To keep above ground tanks in place during the storm secure them by anchoring them, then refill them with either product or water.

Refill the gas tanks to power fire pumps as well as emergency generators.

Check to make sure the fire suppression system operating.

Ensure that important documents are safe either by duplicates or keep them in a safe place away from the site.

Switch off the power to equipment that is not critical and stop any processes that are in production. Fire pumps and sump pumps are two examples of vital equipment that is required to remain in operation.

If the pipe explodes in the midst of a storm, switch off all liquid, gas or pipes that can be ignited.

Please remove all workers.

Make sure you make sure to secure small outbuildings, sheds or others that could not be windproof. Anything you do not wish to be swept away during a storm must be moved in. In the event of a storm, objects such as benches, storage for your yard and plants urns, chairs signs, pots, and flower pots could become particles of debris flying around and cause harm.

A Strategy For Hurricane Recovery

The planning to deal with after a catastrophe will ensure that you're equipped with the appropriate personnel and equipment to assist during your process of recuperation. Choose the most important personnel that you'll require for your recovery prior to the event. Utilize your employee call lists to monitor everyone after the storm has gone away for their security. After that, you can put together your recovery team, and begin working towards getting the business to its feet.

The people who are skilled at repairing plumbing, electrical, mechanical and fire protection systems, along with general maintenance staff for cleanup is required on the team for recovery. The team leader should be designated to be accountable to ensure that the team is equipped with the tools, cleaning equipment, and spare parts that they need. The leader of the team should examine the cause of harm and formulate an action plan based on these priorities as the first priority.

Risks to your safety like power lines that are down and exposed electrical wires as well as gas leaks.

Structures with weak or foundations that are weak.

Alarms and fire alarm equipment that are in need of maintenance.

In order to resume production, vital manufacturing equipment and stock are essential.

Completed emergency repairs ensure safe access to the building.

The rehabilitation team must also follow the steps below:

Set strict safety rules that include a formal hot work permit system for all welding and cutting.

Get rid of any unneeded ignition sources and enforcing "No Smoking" laws.

Develop a method for cleaning off debris that has accumulated from storms or construction work.

If it's safe and secure to do so, patch any holes or damages to the roof of your building.

Assess the salvability of damaged items prior to deciding on repair or replacement.

Make sure you take photos or video of any damaged area.

The team that will be assisting the recovery have to check and fix system of sprinklers and security alarms as well as fire alarms, and also inform the fire department in case one of these systems becomes unusable.

Be cautious when doing electrical repairs, and prior to turning the electrical power on, electricians should have checked, dried properly and tested the systems and devices. The insulation that is wet needs to be removed and removed and replaced. Check for leaks and damages and the necessary drying and cleaning is required for all mechanical equipment and equipment. Furthermore, the source of the water is required to be checked to determine if there is any possibility of contamination.

# Chapter 6: 11 Things You Must Never Do In The Event Of A Hurricane

The impact of hurricanes can be fatal. Use this information to be prepared for the coming hurricane!

Create a hurricane plan

If you reside on the Gulf of Mexico or the Eastern Seaboard, you are well aware that hurricane season is not a joke. Making plans and preparations are crucial to keeping your family members safe. If your local community issue evacuation notices, follow professional advice to relocate your pet, family as well as important papers to a safe location. Take note that being prepared for the storm is risky, especially when you opt to stay at home in the event of a hurricane, even though you're not required to evacuate. However, if you make appropriate precautions, use your common sense and avoid doing these 11 actions during a hurricane You'll be more secure.

During A Hurricane, Avoid Going Outside.

The cat was killed out of curiosity. You could be stricken by it as well. The winds of a hurricane can travel at speeds up to 200 miles per hour, and at these speeds, even tiny fragments of debris could be dangerous. Stay inside until the winds calm down, and don't get fooled by the appearance of calm once the storm's eye is over your head. The winds pick up speed quickly and then move in the opposite direction after the eye has passed. So, you should resist the temptation to try and test the winds.

Laptops, Microwaves, And Other Devices Should Not Be Used.

Appliances and electrical appliances that have been plugged in to power outages could be at risk. To safeguard yourself against interruptions to power in the event of a storm, as well as potential surges when service is restored, turn off devices that are delicate like computers. If there is a chance of flooding backup your electronics in the cloud, then turn off the main circuit breaker but don't try doing the latter if you must walk through the floodwaters for access to the box for breaker.

Don't Film Or Watch A Hurricane From A Window

Or if possible, at all! Broken glass or debris flying around could cause serious damage. Before the storm is even afoot put up a window guard and, when the storm is brewing, keep clear of windows, doors or any other places that could be blown by wind debris. Also, stay clear of looking upwards through the skylight although it may appear to be safe.

During A Hurricane Or Storm, Avoid Taking A Shower.

Lightning strikes can occur in a storm, but they're not often seen in storms. In the event of a hurricane, you should avoid having a bath or washing your hands or washing dishes as they can get into your house via the plumbing system. A misplaced position in the wrong time can cause a lightning strike to be fatal.

Stay Away From External Walls While A Hurricane Is Approaching.

Windows and doors typically protrude across walls that can be a problem when a storm hits. Be as close to the middle of your building as you can, since the frame of your house safeguards spaces inside, such as bathroom and closets.

Wait Until You Receive The All-Clear Signal Before Heading Outside.

Following a storm, take care. A quick departure from your shelter can be disastrous. There is a risk of leaving into the worst storm if your belief is that the calm of the eye of the hurricane to mean the end to the storm. Although the storm may have been completely gone, leaving until the final word is received puts you at risk of fallen power lines, trees and even downed power lines. As long as firefighters, police or even government officials advise you to leave, remain in your place.

Never Use A Cellphone Or Place Calls On One.

The calls are not likely to be answered during the storm, and they could clog the lines and signaling for those that are in actual need of help. Naturally, you should dial 911 when there's an actual emergency be aware that storms can significantly slow response times.

In A Hurricane, Avoid Using A Grill.

Everyone needs to eat. But make sure to keep grills that use gas or charcoal, generators or propane camp stoves outdoors. These all release dangerous carbon monoxide that quickly gets trapped in sealed areas. Make sure to eat only food that is not cooking as well as wrap in blankets, coats and jackets.

If You Haven't Already Found One, Resist The Urge To Begin Looking For A Flashlight.

Prior to the storm, locate an emergency flashlight. Don't wait for a storm to begin before looking in search of your torch. In the event that the wind is uproaring and the waters are moving towards the entry point and you're not sure if you want to be searching for your flashlight in a hurry. When a hurricane is about to make its landfall, ensure you have batteries, flashlights as well as food and other essential items in your arsenal.

Stay Away From Gas Stations.

Get your fuel ready for the storm. If a hurricane is expected to hit be sure to avoid going to the gas station. The gas stations may already be closed and, if power is not on then the pumps will not function also. A crucial job that has to be done prior to a storm's arrival is this. When you are preparing for the storm, make sure you keep your tank of petrol full in order in order to prevent being forced to leave with just half a tank with not having the ability to fill it to capacity.

Do Not Disobey Instructions To Evacuate.

When a storm hits early in the season there is a risk that increases instantly. Take note of the road closing warnings and follow the recommendations from your local authorities. Do not attempt crossing the road that is flooded. Make sure your windows are closed at home, prepare the emergency equipment, and prepare plans for an emergency ahead of time. If an evacuation order is issued, obey the instructions and relocate into a more secure area.

## Chapter 7: 21 Smart Steps That You Can Make

Find out how you can stay secure as well as protect your family members and property from possible disaster in the calm period just before the raging hurricane.

Get ready ahead of time

The threat of hurricanes is a constant one for Southern coastal areas. However, that doesn't mean you must be in constant worry in anticipation of the next hurricane to strike. When hurricane season is approaching There are plenty of inexpensive and simple actions you can adopt to protect your family and secure your home from damage.

Don't be afraid, but stay calm.

The hurricanes are extremely powerful tropical cyclones. They are classed as Category-1 storms based on of sustained winds up to up to 74 miles per hour (based in the SaffirSimpson Hurricane Wind Scale which ranges from 1-5). On a typical year, there are approximately twelve named storms, six hurricanes and three significant storms. In 2020 there were 21 named storms of the Atlantic basin were used, and nine storms were assigned Greek names. As per the National Oceanic and Atmospheric Administration 7 of these storms caused catastrophic damage which cost billions of dollars (NOAA).

While the north Atlantic's hurricane season is from June 1 through October 30, treacherous storms may begin to form in the beginning of May, and can even appear at the end of December. It is a good thing that we now get a variety of alerts due to the hurricane warning programs. There is a chance of flooding or severe storms that produce hurricane-force winds even if you're not close to the sea. You'll be more prepared for a storm in case you live in the area and you are taking the proper steps.

Be aware of your region's storm surge danger

Contrary to common belief the fact is that hurricanes do not only happen near the coast. If tropical storms or coastal storms land then they head inland and bring along storm surges, violent downpours and tornadoes as well as flooding. Storms' moisture content can cause intense rainfall, which can extend to regions in the interior.

The storm surge, which is an impressive increase in the sea's level following an event, is most often the cause for deaths related to hurricanes within the US. Because of secondary flooding in nearby lowland or rivers the storm surges could cause power interruptions and other interruptions in utilities that can restrict your ability to exit your area, or call emergency service.

To determine how prone your area is, and to get the printed or online version of the official plans being implemented to handle flooding in your region Contact the nearest Federal Emergency Management Agency (FEMA) office, or Red Cross chapter.

Know the definitions and hurricane-related terminologies related to hurricanes.

The degree of danger for your area is determined using terms that are used by meteorologists and forecasters. A location is considered to be under "hurricane warning" if a storm that has sustained winds of 74mph or greater is about to land there. This warning will be sent out 36 hours prior to the time that tropical storm force conditions are anticipated to commence. In the event that water levels are at the level of danger warnings may remain present. The chapters that conclude the book have an explanation of the most important terms used in hurricanes that can help.

In the event that storms with sustained wind speeds that are 74 mph and higher are expected within an zone and a "hurricane watch" is issued. The watches are released within 48 hours of when tropical storm force conditions are predicted to commence.

Make a contingency plan for the evacuation

No matter if you reside in an area that is prone to hurricanes or not, an evacuation plan for your family is essential. If the family members don't get together when the storm strikes or are dispersed during the hurricane, your plan should contain a scheduled location for the meeting. Be sure to test the place of meeting and go over your family's local evacuation routes together, and show everyone how the emergency kit is in the emergency kit.

Know Your Hurricane Evacuation Route

There will be an established route to exit in case in the event of an evacuation emergency. Install the FEMA application to get a list of nearby shelters accessible during a natural disaster and also to find the evacuation routes you can take in the event an emergencies. This information reflects the current emergency conditions in your region and is frequently updated by authorities.

In order to avoid being power-less during emergencies, make sure you're equipped with battery backups for your mobile phone. Make copies of the evacuation route's physical maps and shelter addresses as well as telephone numbers in case of need.

Make an "disaster supply kit".

Your emergency kit must be kept in a secure bag, which is waterproof. It can take you with you to evacuations or contain important items if you opt to stay in your home. The amount of emergency kit is contingent on the size of your family and the needs of each family member however, make sure that you have an adult who can carry all the items effortlessly. Make sure you have multiple bags available should you require. It is important that everyone in the family is aware of the place of the bag and it's stored in a safe place.

It is highly recommended that the bag is packed with food items that are nonperishable as well as a first aid kit, additional batteries and a whistle dust mask, sheeting of plastic and duct tape, damp towels, garbage bags, nylon ties, pliers or pliers (to switch off utility services) as well as a manual opener, maps for your local area and a mobile phone that has batteries and chargers, a backup battery along with money.

Be sure to bring all the essentials for your pet and also if you own any. Be sure to take prescription medication and other prescriptions, as well as important financial or family documents along with these essential requirements. Discover more information about preparing an evacuation plan for your house.

Collect nonperishable items.

It's an excellent idea to have a stock of foods that are nonperishable for your emergencies kits. In order to reduce anxiety and crowds Buy nonperishables before you need them instead of just waiting for a storm to be coming towards your location. Choose foods that do not require the preparation of refrigeration or lots of water.

Make sure to include bottles of water, protein or fruit bars, dried cereal peanut butter, dried fruits crackers, nuts and canned items such as fruit, meats and even vegetables (if appropriate). In addition to an emergency supply kit store the items in securely sealed metal or plastic containers that are kept stored in a dry, cold place.

Each six-month period, you should check the water and food items and replace any that have been used up. Every year, you should review your needs and modify the contents of your bag as family demands change.

Take Stock of Water

Strong winds from hurricanes as well as flooding may damage wastewater treatment facilities in municipal areas which can cause water shortages as well as contaminated water in taps. Katrina, the hurricane Katrina affected over 200 wastewater treatment facilities across Mississippi, Louisiana, and Alabama in 2005.

You should ensure you have sufficient drinking water to the whole household for at least 3 days in order to be prepared for the possibility of a water shortage. It is recommended that you keep water on hand for at least three days. Red Cross and FEMA advise drinking one gallon of water for each person every day. So, a family of four requires at minimum 12 gallons of water bottled in the refrigerator at all times.

Get a emergency radio

The emergency kit you have to put in place should contain the hand-crank or battery-powered radio, irrespective of whether every person is in the household with smartphones. If you cannot access your mobile phone, internet, or even energy radios will provide warnings about weather conditions and other important details. A weather-related radio must be bought; it will be able to notify you, even when you turn off the radio or positioned on an alternative channel.

Prepare your pet for their arrival

In preparing for storms, be aware of your dog's need. Make sure they have access to leashes and carriers, as well as food and medications. Leashing or crate-crated to ensure safety as well as control are the best method to ensure your pet's safety as they are subject to stress when they are in an emergency. Be sure that your pet is micro-chipped, and that they have the most current collar tags to protect them in the event of separation. If you are preparing for hurricanes be aware of your dog's needs.

Have easy access to their leashes, carriers and along with medication and food. Crates or leashes to ensure safety and control is a great means to safeguard your animal's security as animals are stressed in times of emergency as well. It is important to ensure that your pets are micro-chipped and have the most current collar tags to protect them in the event of a separation.

Check the insurance contract(s)

Flooding is usually not covered under standard homeowners' insurance policies. The insurance typically covers only damage caused by tropical storm winds and rain regardless of whether or not it is caused by the natural disaster or not.

There are separate flood insurance policies offered. Learn about the coverage offered under your policy through reading the policy, and then adding additional insurance as needed.

Recognize Your Flood Risk

The effects of hurricanes are not just strong winds that cause damage as well as storm surges which can cause floods to the inland regions and coastal properties. This is why it is crucial to know if your house is situated in an area at risk of flooding ahead of the time when hurricane season begins.

There are numerous regionally specific flood maps available online. Contact your insurance company and request that you include flood insurance on the insurance policy for your home if it is deemed to be in moderate or even very high danger of flooding.

Fortify Your Properties

It is important to implement smart home maintenance strategies that minimizes the damage caused by storms, flooding, and high winds. Cleaning out blocked downspouts and gutters so that water has a an easy way to drain out of your home. Take away your patio umbrellas, portable furniture. Store out of season items. Be sure that there aren't any obstacles in the paths as well as access points.

If you're planning to put up a board on windows and doors in order to shield them from the force of hurricane winds, consider making permanent storm shutters, or buying 1/2-inch marine lumber which is made to be cut to suit the windows and doors of your home. It is also a good idea to be prepared with plywood to be prepared in the event of a storm.

Select a secure room

Choose the space in your home that's the most secure location to stay when a hurricane hits in case you plan to stay until the storm passes or you are not able to escape. The lowest floor of the interior space of the house, free from skylights or doors made of glass are the best place for seeking safety, as per FEMA.

It's the best for your family and you to remain in the basement, if there's no possibility of flooding. The most secure area of an apartment without a basement usually is a bathroom or closet.

Write down the shutoffs for your utilities.

The effects of hurricane damage could be electrical surges, cracks in pipelines for water and gas, as well as floods, electric explosions and fire dangers. Look for the gas, water and power shutoffs to ensure you are able to quickly switch the utilities off in case of need.

When you flip the switch for the main circuit breaker inside the electrical box that is usually located within the garage, basement or in a utility closet, it is possible to switch off electricity to your home. The majority of homes contain a main water valve located in the basement, an outside utility space or in an area for storage. Make use of a wrench to turn the valve for shutoff by the gas meter that is on the exterior of the home in the off position, for shutting off a gas line.

Make sure to fill up the tank prior to a storm

Make sure you don't run out of gas during an evacuation. Check that your vehicle is well-fueled and is ready for travel. There is no harm in bringing another petrol container as evacuations may lead to you being waiting in traffic without access to gas stations. Before you start, however you should check the local regulations concerning the secure storage of gasoline.

Make sure your car is secured

Your car is at risk to the hazards which a hurricane can bring in terms of downed trees and branches, power lines, flood water, and all debris that may be blown into the air in the absence of a garage for it to park within.

Though it's not possible to eliminate all hazards to your car but you can limit risks by putting it in a place that's likely to not flood, and away from electrical and tree lines. If you can it is possible to park the vehicle on the downwind aspect of the house to protect it from winds-blown debris. If you take these steps it will reduce the chance that your vehicle could be damaged in the storm. Also, make sure you are prepared to go if you are required to go away.

Travel smart if you must

The act of traveling during or shortly during severe weather conditions is highly dangerous. The majority of those injured by the Hurricane Matthew from North Carolina in 2016 died in vehicles that were flooded in the floodwaters. Actually, driving through flooding causes around 95 deaths each year across the United States. Make sure you avoid often flooded roads since floods often follow storms. Do not drive through an area where it is flooding as it's difficult to know the depth of the water that is murky.

Keep Perishable Foods Safe

Power outages are often caused by hurricanes which means that unless you own the power of a generator, you'll not be in a position to keep food chilled.

# Chapter 8: A Dictionary Of Hurricane Terms

The terminology employed by meteorologists is vital in order to ensure that you are prepared for storms that are coming this year, which are characterized by extreme global climatic changes. The alphabetical list of words used to define tropical storms can be found below.

ACE Accumulated Cyclone Energy ACE, also known as ACE which is an abbreviation. The term is used to describe the intensity and duration of tropical cyclones. Scientists are able to use it evaluate seasons and storms to each other and also between different seasons. The ACE for a particular season is determined by combining the ACE of every storm that occurs during the season. It is calculated by taking into consideration the intensity of their combined duration as well as the quantity.

Cone of Uncertainty Also known as an error cone is a cone-shaped image added to tropical storm track maps, which shows the forecast's error. From the point of prediction 0 hours until the length of the forecast timeframe the cone is extended on each side of the projected track. To show an error in forecast accuracy it is usually smaller at the start of the forecast time.

But, as the forecast timeframe advances into the future, the error in forecasting grows and the cone gets wider. It is calculated based upon the error rates of forecasts for the storms of the last five years and does not reflect the meteorology specific to a particular storm. There is a common misconception that tropical cyclone's impacts (storm surge, rain, as well as wind) are restricted to that region within the cone. The truth is that these effects may extend to many thousands of miles beyond the cone. The cone will shrink because forecast accuracy keeps getting more precise.

Convection involves the process of transferring moisture and heat from upper layers of atmosphere into the upper layer by air moving currents. Clouds form by the cooling of rising air and then condenses. The rain will form when there is sufficient water. It is sometimes perceived as a storm that is contained in the storm.

Cyclones are a massive rotational storm that has an initial area that is low in pressure. Storm power and the winds grow as the pressure in the core drops. The wind is drawn upwards and downwards by the rotating pressure. The result is that thunderstorms appear and to grow in strength.

Despite that due to the climate conditions, cyclones can be very rare within the

Southern Hemisphere, cyclones revolve in a cyclonical manner (counter-clockwise) within the Northern Hemisphere and anti-cyclonically (clockwise) within the Southern Hemisphere.

Diverse ocean basins use different designations for cyclones. For example, they are referred to as hurricanes within the Atlantic and Eastern Pacific as well as typhoons that occur in the western Pacific as well as tropical cyclones within the Indian Ocean and South Pacific.

Data collection is a crucial part of forecasting tropical storms. Through the duration of a specific storm, planes perform drones to conduct aerial reconnaissance missions and collect information. They are the National Oceanographic and Atmospheric Administration as well as the Air Force are responsible for the execution of these activities within the United States (NOAA).

They can be flown in the midst of a storm, over the storm, and drop devices inside to collect data on the direction of wind and speed, as well as temperature, the humidity and pressure at various altitudes in the air.

UAVs, also known as unmanned aircraft vehicles (UAVs) that have a longer capability of time-aloft and range can be used to observe distant ocean areas because of the restricted capabilities of the manned aircraft. Helicopters, ships and weather buoys and low-altitude uni-purpose UAVs as well as satellites, radar as well as unmanned watercrafts are all able to collect information.

The eye of a storm is the central point. The air inside a central cyclone will recede when it gets stronger (while the atmosphere rises inside the remainder of the cyclone). The warm air rises and sinks, dispersing clouds, and precipitation because of it. Cyclones with greater force often feature clouds that are high and clear. They are observed from above, completely obscure the eyes. The eyewall, located just outside the eye is where the most intense storms as well as powerful winds form an area around the eye. The highest-pitched thunderstorms as well as the strongest winds and the most heavy rainfall can occur inside the eyewall.

The center of a storm is clouds of storms, and lines of cloud that are dense and brimming with water. They often look like spirals while the cyclone is rotating. The clouds that form these bands that radiate outwards from the central area of the cyclone and extend for several miles, may be related to extremely intense rain. The low-level cloud lines that get dragged by the current updraft that is forming in a thunderstorm are referred to as feeder bands, but on a smaller size.

A hurricane is a Atlantic tropical cyclone with wind speeds that are sustained by at least seventy-four miles an hour (119 km/h). There are a variety of reasons and environmental variables that could trigger the development of tropical cyclones.

The warm ocean is vital for the formation process as it causes the surrounding environment to become unstable, and causes the humidity to increase in temperature. The typical water temperature ranges from 80 to 82 degrees (26oC) however it is possible for cyclone formation to occur in warmer seas.

An environment that permits the warm air to cool off as it ascends is essential for its development. It becomes increasingly unstable due to the release of heat, which can also allow clouds, raindrops and storms to develop. In addition both the upper and mid levels need to be steady in order for thunderstorms to grow in a vertical direction without being ripped apart by wind. In order to allow cyclone development an unsettling area weather of any kind or even a single wave that is low pressure, needs to eventually move into the environment.

The season during which hurricanes are the most likely to be observed is known as the season of hurricanes. Between June 1 and November 30, Atlantic, Caribbean, and Gulf of Mexico are all susceptible to storm activity. This occurs within the Eastern Pacific Basin between May 15 until November 30. It is the Central Pacific hurricane season lasts between June 1 and November 30. Yet, hurricanes could be seen outside the window. Actually this year, the Atlantic Basin has seen at most one tropical storm every month during the year. The season of typhoons is believed to occur all year round throughout the west Pacific.

If a tropical or hurricane storm hits land the eye (or the center) moves inland before crossing the shoreline. But, this doesn't necessarily suggest that the storm "struck land" for the first time since the bands of rain that produce torrential rainfall and powerful winds generally appear several hours, or days before.

Additionally, in the days leading up to the arrival of the eye, the seas along the coast could begin to increase, which could cause catastrophic damage. Multiple landfalls may be the result of a single storm. In the event that a storm crosses an island or shifts course, it may be able to re-emerge on the ocean and then make subsequent landfalls in various locations.

One of the numerous elements used by meteorologists in predicting tropical change is the Madden-Julian oscillation (MJO). The higher-frequency phase of the MJO is distinguished by the presence of specific areas of active storms which are moving between east and west throughout the equatorial region of the globe. It is important for forecasting because it indicates a greater probability of tropical development The prediction of tropical development can be made with greater confidence because the MJO is monitored and its movements anticipated. The National Center of Atmospheric Science's Roland Madden and Paul Julian discovered the MJO in the year 1971.

A hurricane's maximum sustained speed that is the Saffir-Simpson Hurricane Scale gives a hurricane one to five. Five categories are employed to determine the potential damage to property:

74-95 miles per hour in category 1. small damage risk

96-110 mph, category 2. considerable damage potential

111-129 mph in category 3. Devastating potential for harm

130-156 mph is the category 4. Risk of catastrophic loss

Anything over an 157mph speed is classified as category 5. Risk of massive destruction

The scale was invented in the year 1971 in 1971 by Robert Simpson, a meteorologist as well as Herbert Saffir, a civil engineer. Important to note that the estimation of storm surge should not be done with this scale. Saffir-Simpson Scale.

Storms and clouds that are spiraling towards the center of a hurricane are called spiral bands.

A severe hurricane or storm will be followed by an apparent elevation of the sea, referred to as storm surge. The large, wind-driven field that circling the center of the storm pushes seawater into coastlines. The intensity of the storm the extent of its wind fields, the location of the coastline and its slope to the ocean bottom all play a role on how strong the storm surge can be, it can reach many feet higher than normal tides. The storm surge can be a significant cause of the majority deaths and injuries caused by tropical cyclones. It is important to note that every place which is susceptible to storm surge is distinct, which makes precise forecasting of storm surge extremely complicated. So, it's essential to follow the guidelines from the local authorities on evacuation and preparation.

The first rise in sea levels before an tropical storm or a hurricane arrives at landfall is called the "set-up tide. Set-up tides gradually increase for up to 2 days prior the landfall date, unlike surge of storms, which typically arrives at the point of landfall, and can be extremely destructive. Set-up tides could cause the closure of the escape routes of low lying areas far before the beginning of the storm. This makes them extremely dangerous.

A tropical storm is categorized by the term tropical depression when its sustained top winds are not more than 39 mph.

The most destructive storms that occur in the world Earth are tropical storms. A storm system called an tropical storm features the ability to sustain surface circulation, and speeds of between 39 and 73 miles/hour. Tropical storms are classified into cyclones and typhoons and hurricanes, based on the place they originate.

A tropical wave is cluster of thunderstorms located in the tropics, which is traveling westward in the low pressure trough. If favorable conditions in the atmosphere are found this tropical storm has the possibility of developing into the tropical depression.

Typhoons are tropical hurricanes that occur in the Northwestern Pacific basin, close to China and the Marshall islands and the Philippines.

## Chapter 9: Attitudes

When a storm strikes and you listen to the news on radio, television or learn about it in newspaper, you read about individuals who were of an attitude of being more powerful and tougher that Mother Nature.

Nature's strength is far greater than anything humans could achieve, even with the most arduous efforts. It is possible to build better and safer homes. And we are able to weather and test everything that we can, but we are still not able to compete to the strength of a hurricane.

There are some people in the world with this type of toughness that makes them believe they're real bad-asses, and no one can stop them from taking everything they own. We've all met them as you've all had the pleasure of meeting their faces and spoken with them.

This approach could lead to your death or, at the bare minimum make your losses worse and leave you in risky situations. Nature and storms are places that even the toughest man with the most willpower could be destroyed quickly by water floods or struck by falling debris.

Although it is not necessary to fear the weather, you need to be aware of the weather. It is important to be aware of the risks involved, and how could be affected by them or your family, as well as your home. Also, set your masculine attitude to the side and contemplate what's most likely to occur.

There's nothing to feel shameful about being worried. Fear is among the mechanisms that our brains employ to stop us from engaging in dangerous or foolish things. It helps us stay away from danger. It ensures that we are safe and secured. If you're faced with risk and you were not just a bit scared this is the time you tend to commit stupid mistakes.

Sometimes, fear may enslave our minds and stop our from doing the tasks that are necessary to ensure our safety. When fear gets so overwhelming that it makes us unable to perform the task that needs to be accomplished, that's a negative circumstance. Therefore, be scared but take action and follow through with what is required.

Another attitude be wary of is the notion that a storm will perform what it's going to do, but we're in no position to end it. Even though this might be some of the time true, what is really happening is that there's a lot that we can take on.

The best way to approach this is in which we realize that something's going to happen, and we're prepared to think about what needs to be accomplished, and then do it with the highest of ability.

There are steps we can take to prevent damage, and also secure our home and belongings. If we do these things and still something happens it is possible to continue without a worry. If we fail to do the little safeguards and major harm is caused as a result of it, we'll need to bear the consequences probably for the rest of our lives.

We must adopt an attitude of not invincible, and that nature and floods, storms or even flooding are much stronger than what we can ever hope to be. You should start telling your self that nature is much stronger than you, and you have nothing to do but to try and show yourself to something greater and better.

If you are able to trust and accept that you are doing it, you stand a an increased chances of surviving every storm healthy and sound.

Listen to Warnings

In the past, people were given a limited information or warnings when floods or storms arrived. 100 years ago, the first indication that something wasn't correct could have been flooding or winds entering the town!

Today, we are blessed with technology which allows us to be aware much in advance, often several weeks ahead, about the onset of a storm or blizzard, or even a flood. This allows us to make steps we must take for the protection of our as well as our family members and even our houses.

The weather reports can provide us with an idea of the likely path that storms will take throughout the world. Through these reports, it is possible to determine which times we need to take proper measures. These days or weeks of advance warning could affect the way, or badly, we perform in situations.

The meteorologists on television and The National Weather Service know what is happening in your local area, and give you that information often throughout the each day. However, this information can only help you if you pay attention to it! If you bury your head into the sand and ignore the warnings and notices it is only hurting your self.

It is crucial to give advance notice because certain things simply cannot be carried out during a time of severe weather. For instance, the idea of putting wood over the doorway would seem impossible and also extremely risky even in winds of 30 mph. The winds could take the plywood sheet straight out of your fingers which could cause injury or property damage.

It is important to have a plan to be prepared for the time the first warnings begin to be issued. If there is a chance of a severe storm for your location, begin the process and begin gathering items that are needed. When the risk becomes more precise and nearer, you'll know what you need to do and what to bring.

Keep in mind that you're not by yourself and there are hundreds of thousands or millions of other people living the location you reside in that share the same dilemma. Therefore, gathering flashlights, batteries as well as other equipment could be difficult, especially if people take the lead and clear the shelves.

Also, you should be aware of where your various supplies are you using in the event of a storm. You should ensure that you are equipped with the equipment and tools required and are easily accessible and well-organized. It's not a good idea for you to waste an hour searching for that cordless drill that you bought just a few months ago, only to discover it's be without a battery!

The warnings provide an estimated timeframe on what conditions could be worsened and the time how soon they will improve. This can help you determine the things you will do in the event of a crisis and plan for alternate accommodations and other necessities.

The warnings also provide specifics on the size and strength of the storm, as well. It's important to know this because methods one can use to prepare in the event of an a Category 4 storm would differ significantly from plans for a Category 1 hurricane.

This will be repeated several times throughout this book since it's extremely real:

Knowledge is Power!

The more you are aware about it, the more you'll be in a position to plan ahead and ensure that all the things that need to be done gets accomplished in time to avoid the storm.

Beware of being lulled by the illusion of safety in the event that the track for the storm is predicted to move away from your location. The tracks used are computer simulations. They are usually precise, there are instances when storms took unintentional turns, or don't take the direction everyone is expecting and continue straight ahead.

If the weather is moving toward you ensure that you're well-prepared. It's always safer to take your mistakes in a safe manner and prepare yourself rather than fall victim to a lack of preparation and pay the negative consequences. An hour of preparation will save you a great deal of heartache and headache to come back later. Additionally, it's simple to complete tasks while not feeling the tension and stress of an approaching storm. It is easier to work with less stress and the work you do will be higher quality.

Safety Warnings

Other types of information that you must take note of is security warnings. They are warnings that your state or local authorities can issue when there is a risky storm could be imminent or likely to occur within your region.

Most often, warnings include warnings about storm conditions and evacuation alerts.

Storm condition warnings are warnings given region by area when the threat of storms approaches. They include warnings for high winds and snow or rain accumulation warnings, and flood advisories. If a warning is given in your local area, this means that these weather conditions have the greatest likelihood of occurring within your region and you must be prepared.

The warnings usually are issued around. 24 hours prior to the majority of weather conditions, except for thunderstorms such as tornadoes that form extremely quickly. If that is the case, alerts might arrive just minutes or even hours ahead of.

Additionally, there are statements referred to as "advisories" hat are issued prior to when conditions favorably in the location. They can be released within 48 hours so that people can get additional time to prepare. As the time gets closer and threats remain then the advisories change into alerts.

Evacuation Warnings

If the conditions are likely to be extreme, or when the occurrence of such conditions is probable the local authorities or the police could issue evacuation notices or the need for evacuations.

Warnings or orders for evacuations are given or placed into place with a specific reason and only for one reason. This is because they are meant to protect people's lives. Although many people believe that evacuation orders were put for the protection of residents but that's only a small part of the purpose. The evacuation orders are put intended to protect firefighters, police and other emergency responding personnel too.

In the event that someone remains in their home, and the conditions get to the point that they are incapable of leaving on their own and find themselves in danger, usually first responders are dispatched to save the people. This means that not only are they put themselves at risk but they're putting the lives of first responders in danger too. Actually certain local authorities implement policies which prohibit first emergency responders from heading to help those that did not leave. This protects the safety of first responders.

If an evacuation has been requested or recommended within your region, you must take a serious look at taking the necessary steps to get out. Don't be one of those who linger in order to "ride out" the storm. Numerous deaths have occurred due to people who did not wish to remain in shelters or somewhere else prior to and during the storm.

These warnings and orders must not be viewed as a joke or implemented without much consideration. These are based on the knowledge and experience of many experts and are based on the information and data from various professional and weather organizations. Don't think that you have more knowledge than the experts do, since you could be mistaken. Perhaps even completely wrong.

Some are concerned that by letting their houses go that they're creating easier for burglars to gain entry and take their belongings. Although that could be the case, there are two factors should be taken into the consideration.

The first thing to do is before the storm comes, zones under evacuation are normally being inspected by police or other organizations looking for those who are doing things they're not expected to be doing. The police are aware of what's happening and they are more focused at what appears to be questionable conduct. Can that guarantee nothing bad will take place? No. It's likely that it's not more serious than you think. In the end, if there is no reason for people to stay there when it is stormy there is a good chance that thieves also stayed in the area.

Another thing to know is that our possessions as well as homes can be substituted. Human lives cannot. It's more beneficial to go home and discover your brand new flat panel television is missing rather than stay inside and end in serious injury or death. It is possible to rebuild your home and even replace the television your jewellery. However, the loss of life, or even an arm or leg from injury is extremely, extremely permanent.

The warnings are in place to safeguard human lives. They give individuals the greatest chance of getting through a hurricane or any other situation with the lowest quantity of disruption and destruction. These are set up in order to allow people the enough time to prepare and react.

These alerts are given by experts who know what's happening and will be the probable consequences to individuals and the region within which they reside. The warnings aren't given in a casual manner. Do warnings occasionally get issued, but there is no response?

Absolutely.

Is it truly more dangerous that the chance? The most common assumption is that if the previous warning was not needed, then it will have the same effect. If nothing occurred this time, nothing is likely to occur this time around either.

If you think this way, you will be more likely to be in danger circumstances. Our area experienced a major storm this year, and evacuation in particular areas were put in the place. Many areas were unaffected and many people were upset.

Just a few months back, another severe storm struck, and evacuation notices were also issued for those regions. The coastal regions affected by the storm were devastated, houses washed away, huge flooding and billions of dollars in damages. A lot of those who were left died, and others put the lives of the emergency personnel in danger as they attempted to save people.

There are warnings to serve a purpose and all is required to be attentive and adhere to their instructions to the letter. It's safer to be secure rather than sorry, no matter how difficult it may be.

Know Your Area!

In the event of severe weather conditions or storms It is essential to learn about the place that you reside. Knowing more about your location, the more you'll be aware of the actions and precautions you should undertake.

If it's extreme storms such as Hurricanes and Nor'easters, areas along the coast are particularly susceptible to flooding and storm surge. flooding. Even inland regions could be at risk of flooding, too. Low lying regions are easily flooded due to overflowing rivers and streams or excessive rainfall.

Thus, every person should possess a fundamental understanding of the place where they live or are residing. You will be aware if you're near the coast or the oceanfront, but those living in the inland regions, you must be aware of local streams and rivers, as well as the height above sea level the area is.

In the case of example, if you live in the countryside with an area of water nearby it's important to be aware of whether your location is greater or less in comparison to the river. If one part of your area is located 50 feet above sea level while another has a height of 5 feet above sea level, it's simple to determine that the 5 feet above sea level area has more at risk of being flooded over the 50-foot region.

However, even that may not be enough, since water is at its lowest and, if it is flowing from an area that is higher than the 50-foot region, it is likely to run across the entire area in order to reach into lower regions. Therefore, it's essential to inquire with your both the state and local governments to find out how your region is assessed or how it ranks against others.

Local and state areas typically have flood zones or maps showing the past performance of floods along with other elements. For coastal regions like the ones in California you will find numbered flood zones that begin near the coastline before moving towards the inland. Based on the intensity of the hurricane, they will determine which areas are most likely to flood and will issue alerts.

**Chapter 10: Evacuation Or Travel**

Another reason you should be aware of your location is in the event that you have to leave or move within the area in the event of a weather or storm associated event. Being aware of which regions are most susceptible to flooding or becoming impervious can be extremely helpful when you decide which path you should take.

Know the top and lowest places of your neighborhood along with areas where shelters or safe places could be in the event that you require these. The information you need is typically available through your town's offices.

If flooding is an issue or even a fact and you are concerned, it's best to be aware of the most dangerous places to be so that you're able to go to a safe place. Do not rely solely on what you think is safe as you may end getting into difficulty. Get someone's help and obtain exact and reliable facts instead of relying on guesswork.

In the coastal regions, there are usually ways to evacuate in an emergency in order to let people move away from the coast to move on more secure levels. It is common to see warning signs along these routes that identify them as an emergency Evacuation Route.

The roads are generally bigger and therefore not subject to flooding in the early stages. These roads also come with parking restrictions under certain conditions as well as being closely monitored or patrolled during emergencies. It is a good thing because in the event that you do be stuck or encounter issues in the future, the last place you'd want to be during an emergency or in a flood is along a tiny roadway to the side of the road!

The local police department is likely to be able inform about the streets and the routes that are in your vicinity in addition to providing more important safety tips about shelters, food sources and water sources when you have to utilize these.

Know Your Limitations!

With regards to weather and preparations for storms it is important to know the limits the world has imposed upon you. They could be physical restrictions or restrictions on the abilities which you've available. Understanding these limitations can aid you in working with greater safety and efficient manner.

As an example the majority of us who are old people are unable to perform certain things we did as children. It's not a negative issue or something we need to be embarrassed or ashamed about. This is just what happens to each of us at some point or the other.

It is a problem in situations where someone who cannot anymore do something believes they're able to complete it. This individual could fall, or suffer another injury while trying to accomplish more than they're able to perform. The person could pull or tear muscles or fall off ladders, among many other undesirable things.

Another problem is the ability. A few people are able to figure out the best way to accomplish almost any task, while some have difficulty understanding how to inject the gas they own into their vehicle. It's not an issue or something to be embarrassed or ashamed about. Every person has strengths and weaknesses, and so you know the things that matter and how to deal with them, we will be able to manage these.

If we are aware of our limits and limitations, we are able to get the job accomplished in a quicker and safe method. It is possible to limit areas we aren't able to accomplish and focus on the things that we can or understand most effectively.

In this case, for instance, I could be able to accomplish some of the duties to safeguard my exterior but I would need to put some plywood to the windows or doors. Perhaps I don't have the tools well, or perhaps the house is three stories which means I'm not comfortable with the ladders or heights. Whatever the cause, as that we're conscious of the issue, we can find someone who can do these tasks for us when it is necessary to do them.

Three scenarios occur when we attempt to accomplish tasks that we don't know how to do or don't know how accomplish. The result is that either we do more harm due to the fact that we aren't sure of is going on or hurt ourselves. Or we perform a poor or unprofessional task.

In the example of plywood If we aren't aware of the use of tools efficiently, we may insert a screw into the window, breaking the glass or harm the frame of the door or window and cause leaks. If we attempt to lift an object that's too heavy and fall over back, strain a muscle or break the object. You could even fall off the ladder while trying to reach this second-story window and suffer a serious injury.

Additionally, if we do not be aware of the best way to ensure the plywood is secured, it can be blown away during storms and damage other property as well as property, and it won't be able to secure our windows and doors the way it is supposed to. Perhaps you screwed screws wrong or didn't choose the proper amount of screws, or different because you're uninformed. No matter the reason the issue will arise. Before you begin any type of preparation for a storm consider what you're able to achieve and whether you are capable of doing. Do your best to be honest with yourself, and be willing to recognize your shortcomings. Doing otherwise could cause you to suffer potentially harmful results.

Once you've completed the list of chores as well as other tasks that have to be completed, mark those that you require assistance in. Find out who could assist you in those tasks or do the work to your satisfaction. Perhaps it's your father or mother or acquaintance or a neighbor. There's a chance that you'll need get someone to take care of these things for you. No matter what the alternatives, work the details out ahead of time.

Make contact with those who can assist you. Inform them of your requirements ahead of time. Inform them that you'll be calling them, so that they know. This is particularly important for situations where you're hiring a person. The person you hire could be booked rapidly, therefore calling them to establish your expectations for the long period is the best idea to make. Contact them as your situation requires for them to be available. Give them as much time as you can.

This is also true for family as well as friends and neighbors. Keep in mind that you're not in this issue on your own. There is a good chance that the work you'll need to be doing on your house is going to need to be completed on their houses too. Give them the some time to assist you and complete what they have to accomplish for themselves too.

While no one wants coming to the realization If you discover that you're no longer able to take proper care of your property and safeguard your home from such scenarios, it may be the right time to engage a service to manage all of your needs if such instances occur frequently, or look into shifting to an place where these issues will no need to be a problem.

Everything discussed in this book were designed to shield the family members, you as well as your belongings from destruction or loss. If you are trying to accomplish things you're not capable of in the first place, you're defeating the purpose behind this book. It is best to put your feelings and ego aside and focus on what's secure and appropriate for you.

It's not something to feel ashamed or embarrassed about. It's just something that the universe has handed to each one of us. We need to change as we move through life.

Insurance

As odd as it may sound the majority of people do not know the extent of their insurance during a natural catastrophe or a storm. It is only in the aftermath of an event after they make an insurance claim, only to discover that they're not insured for the type of injury.

One of the most frequently encountered difficulties is the flood. Certain areas have homeowner insurance will not be able to provide coverage for flood damages. This is usually the case for areas that are classified as areas with a high risk of flooding. Ironically, there isn't enough coverage that you require most.

Most of the time, you are able to get separate flood damage insurance that is federally subsidized or funded. However, you should check with your insurance provider and carefully read the policy to ensure you're secure from flood damages.

Another aspect that lots of people are unaware of is the fact that during the event of a hurricane, you could face an enormous additional deductible is required to pay before the insurance company will cover the damaged.

This deductible for hurricanes takes effect when a storm has reached an amount, size or any other condition. If any of the conditions are fulfilled then the deductible is activated. If you are a victim of the deductible, confirm the criteria which determine the time it will kick into.

In some cases, those criteria do not need to be satisfied in the area you reside, but any state which you are located. This means that you could be required to cover the higher tax deductible due to an area that is several hundred miles away fulfilled the requirements, but not yours. Take a look at the fine print within the policy you have purchased and get your agent to clarify what does not make sense.

To ensure that the insurance policy is valid, ensure that the information within the policy is current in date and correct. Sometime, changes happen to the house and your insurance policy has not been changed. In the event, you file a claim. The coverage will be decreased because the changes or modifications were not disclosed.

Finally, ensure that the insurance policies you've purchased are fully paid, and you don't have unpaid or delayed payments. If your insurance premium is due soon and you are anticipating a severe storm make sure you send the payment delivered to your address so that you can make sure that it is received and the account is up-to-date. Don't give any reason for anyone to deny an insurance policy or to deny insurance coverage.

The amount of coverage you receive should be changed as the location of your residence and belongings alter. If you purchase additional or larger items of value it is possible that you will over the sum you are insured for to cover the replacement of those things. Although your insurance premium is likely to be higher as coverage increases, it is important to know precisely what you're insured for to ensure there will there won't be any unexpected costs.

To safeguard your rights and the property you own To protect your property and interests, we strongly recommend to go out before the storm is expected to hit and snap photos of your home from every angle and also your home. This can prove the absence of any prior damages before the storm. If there is something that shows the time of the storm (like newspapers) it could be useful also.

If there are any damage, make sure you capture photos of the destruction. Sometimes, utility companies or city workers may come by to remove fallen trees and other objects to clear roads. This could cause damage to your property, and cause doubts about what exactly transpired. The photos immediately afterward will provide the real picture of destruction.

Although the majority of insurance firms are trustworthy and have employee inspectors and adjusters have integrity and are willing to help However, there are some that are not, and it is essential to safeguard yourself from these types of people.

After the storm take thorough inspections and tests and identify everything that suffered damage. Make a note of the damage and snap photos. The adjuster will examine the list and conduct the inspection themselves. If they can come up with all the information, it's wonderful. If they overlook something you have discovered Bring them to the subject by presenting it in a professional manner, and request them to verify the damages.

Insurance is a service we purchase that will help us to rebuild and restore our houses and lives. The most efficient way to make use of insurance is to properly ensure yourself, and then ensure that your interests are taken into consideration when you settle. This means understanding the risks you're covered against, what rights you're legally entitled to, and how you can get what you're entitled to.

**Chapter 11: Basic Storm Safety**

In the case of the weather and storms as well as other problems, safety must be the top priority. Even though our houses and possessions are valuable, these things are able to be repaired, but human lives aren't. Keep in mind that security should always be our top priority. Every action we take should improve the level of our personal or safety of our families. If not, then we need to be focused on completing other activities first.

As we discuss our houses and making them the most secure they can be in the other chapters in this book, it's important to realize that our homes, except for the time you need to leave they will remain our main source of safety and shelter.

It doesn't mean every place in your home are safe. There some areas in your house which are more secure than other areas, especially during extreme storms such as major storms or tornadoes.

If there's a storm that brings the wind, it is advised to stay from the outside walls of the house, particularly the windows and doors. Glass is one of the weakest parts of the wall when is exposed to flying debris, so nobody should be on the window in order to view the storm. This could be extremely risky with branches and blowing debris from the wind flying about. The debris can hit an unprotected window and crack completely through, injuring those who are standing there.

As glass-related injuries is often devastating, it's best to secure blinds and drapes so that you can limit the area glass could go in the event of a break. Shut all doors inside and windows to ensure that wind-blown glass can't leave the room that has the damaged window.

The windows that are commonly called "hurricane glass" that have the special membrane of plastic that is sandwiched between two pieces glass. This membrane is created to permit glass to break upon impact, but the membrane prevents most objects from entering your home.

Although this glass offers an enormous safety benefit and a significant improvement over regular glass, it shouldn't create the illusion of safety as if it's safe to sit on the windowsill when there is a strong wind. This could lead to death-defying or potentially life-threatening.

Be sure that the windows and doors are secure and locked. You will experience an increase in tension difference between the interior of the home and outside, and this may cause locked doors and windows to wide. Make sure to lock doors and install deadbolts in the event that you have.

The ideal spots to stand is under stairs or inside doorways. These are because these areas have massive overhead supports that are designed to hold the weight of ordinary walls. Although nothing can guarantee the safety of your family members if you are hit by a vehicle onto your house, standing within the safest areas of your house will increase the odds.

Also, it is important to observe the manner in which wind is moving. This will allow you to know what trees and objects could fall on the home, and then you are able to ask everyone to head toward the opposite direction. In the case of example, if winds are blowing toward the front of your home The trees that are in front are likely to drop in the direction of the wind blows, and this would mean that they will fall towards the house.

However, in the rear of the home, those trees could fall of the property, which makes that space more safe than those in front. It is true that if the tree which will fall is sufficiently large, the area is guaranteed to be secure, however we're making the safest option when faced with a risk. Even though nothing can be guaranteed to ensure security but we can increase the odds by taking smart decision.

Many people believe that the tub is the best place for a bath since you can lay down inside it, and be sheltered from the sides of the bathtub. When the bathtub is plastic one, your protection will probably be lower than if it was one of the older cast iron tubs that were used for in the past. The drawback of being in the bathtub is that could not be possible to get out if there were to fall over. While you may be able to escape injuries, you may end in a position of being trapped and not be able to get out of the home.

If you are trapped in a situation, it's always best to be in an area that offers several ways to escape. A house, for instance, must have the back and front doors, and be able to use the front or back doors from wherever you're. If something is blocking the exit you want to use, you will be able to easily exit using the second exit.

One of the challenges of staying in an upper level or in a basement. Most often, the access to the basement, or even upper floors can be reached by only one staircase. If there's a secondary entrance in the basement or an additional staircase from the upper floors it's a good idea. Make sure you have at least two options for exiting.

Always keep a flashlight close to your at all times. There is no way to know when electricity will stop working and you may be caught totally dark. An emergency flashlight will assist you to locate ways to free yourself and get to a safer location. Additionally, it will help find others who might have been trapped in.

If you're a parent and you have children, it's important to ensure for everyone to knows how to act and how to get there in the event of an crisis. This could include losing power, water, fire or other disasters. There should be a plan that you practice at least once a year to ensure that people don't need to consider how to proceed, but simply do it. This is particularly important when you have children under the age of five who could be separated from their parents during the event.

Inform everyone that they must meet at an outdoor place in the event of an emergency with a fire. Let everyone know where to take refuge in the event of extreme winds, such as hurricanes or tornadoes. There are likely to be several locations for various events. Make sure to cover all of them and thoroughly explain the reasons behind them. Reread and ask questions to children to be sure that they comprehend.

During times of high stress, the people living are in the residence should remain within close proximity of each other. It will be easier to act and also keep track of the location of everyone. Be sure not to be down at home in the basement while your children play in the 3rd floor. Gather everyone and enjoy games, go to the TV, or just do things with your family.

Certain types of storms, including hurricanes, contain an area of calm that is known as"eye" "eye" of the storm. The eye is where the winds decrease and the skies may even unobstructed for a few minutes. Make sure to be cautious as the eye's area is quite small, and when it is gone the winds of storms will come back to reverse direction. If you have to go outside to inspect things take it quickly and cautiously. It is not a good idea to be in the area when problems start to flare getting back to normal.

During an eye or calm, it is not the right opportunity to take out the ladder to reattach the plywood or make other repair. Return inside and allow the storm to go away.

Make sure that children remain inside until the storm has cleared the region. After that, it is recommended to take an adult out and check the place to be sure the area is secure before taking children outside. Children will be interested and would like to check out how the outside appears. Parents should take children out and talk about what transpired.

Do not scare the kids, but instead, explain the reasons why this kind of weather and storms should be treated with respect for their incredible force. Our children should learn to respect the power of nature as well as the forces behind it.

Memories

When we are thinking of being able to lose things, we often imagine our possessions. Our cars, our homes or furniture, these are but a small sample of the things that we usually consider. For those who've been through an extreme storm and suffered losses other types of property is often what comes to the forefront.

Our stories.

It's amazing to think that we invest all of our time and energy to protect physical items, yet we forget to protect the memories of the lives we lived that led us here.

Ask storm victims if they suffered the loss of their homes or saw them badly damaged. One of the items that are most often mentioned while crying is the photos and other mementos of their lives that are in the past for good. We should therefore give an idea of how we can keep and safeguard these memories.

There is no way to ensure our complete security or our property. Mother Nature will get her way eventually and there's not much that we can do to prevent her from doing it constantly. However, that doesn't mean that you have to stop the efforts completely. In the case of personal possessions we possess There are a variety of options that we can take to protect those things we treasure and can't be substituted.

Images can be stored in containers that are waterproof and then secured against flooding. Also, they can be kept on the top floors of your home, such as the second and third floors. If the first floor is flooded, those things could be saved.

The majority of pictures we take are stored in digital formats and may be stored on CD-ROM discs that are, at a minimum, resistant to the effects of water. An external hard drive is able to be stored in a container that is waterproof. In fact, even a weather resistant safe is a good way to protect those precious memories.

Even though you won't be able to save the all 30 feet wall of sports awards your kids have collected throughout their education You can get rid of those diplomas from college or other important documents to box them up and relocate them away to a safe place.

The best option is to gather important documents and photos and relocate them to another area, like a family member's residence that's located on a higher level. In the event that the threat is really real and massive then you can hire a storage facility and transfer all your essential items elsewhere.

It's true that this takes time and effort, but often the work you put in will turn out ineffective once the threat is gone. The mere thought of losing your memories that are dear and dear to you ought to cause you to make the necessary steps that you must take to safeguard the things that are most important to you.

Here are some ideas on ways you can protect your memory and increase your chances to last through in the event of a hurricane:

Transfer items into more elevated levels of the ground

Place items in containers that are weatherproof

Important items should be moved to a different place

Digital information such as images as well as documents on a Web hosting server.

It's also a smart idea to make sure you have all important papers and other memorabilia all in one spot in case you need to get out or go about your business fast, you will be able to get them to leave. If the wind is ripping out windows, or when flooding waters are threatening to fill the road, that's not a good best time to look for objects and then securing things up!

There are many safe and waterproof containers to protect your precious memories. The only thing you need to do is give it some thought and perform some research.

People don't always think about this until it's already too late, and the pictures and their memories have disappeared forever.

Medical Issues

It is essential to think about the medical needs of the people in relation to weather. As the requirements of patients remain despite storms it is essential to ensure that their needs are enough to satisfy them at a minimum for a specific period of time.

The first step is for those who have severe or complex medical issues should be moved to an area that is safe where they will continue receiving the support, treatment and medical care they require. The facilities and manpower available may not be accessible after the storm is over and in the aftermath.

If you are aware of someone who has an issue that could be serious to their health look into the different options available to use in an emergency. The local police or fire departments are able to give that details to you quickly.

Individuals with less significant medical conditions or requirements could be able at home or in the region, however they must have someone around to supervise them and ensure that they are well taken well. This could be achieved through family members or friends. If no family members are nearby maybe the individual could be in a nearby house in the midst of a storm. They can then go back home, with a limited amount of check-ins following the storm's end.

It's also crucial to recognize that medical staff may not be available in the aftermath of a storm since they may be transferred or required elsewhere to tend the storm's victims. Be aware that massive power interruptions and failure of communication could lead to the closure of office hours as well as elective surgeries.

This means that patients should plan their medical needs before they learn of a storm that is coming. If you've got an appointment planned during or after the storm, maybe they will be able to fit into the appointment before. Office staff might be grateful for this since it can ease their workload in the aftermath of the storm. You may want to change your schedule prior to the storm's arrival in order in order to secure the most convenient following storm-related appointments. These appointments will get booked quickly therefore, the sooner you make an appointment your better could be.

For those who use regular medication It is important to ensure there is enough medicine on the shelf to last us through the storm, and for a adequate amount of time to recover from the storm. It could be necessary to refill a prescription prior to the arrival of the storm. Remember that the power outages could shut down pharmacies during unspecified lengths of time. You can take a break from your supplements for a week, but not the diabetic or heart medication!

Be sure that all medicines are clearly labeled bottles, and stored in a outdoor container or bag. This can help to ensure that they are safe in the event that water should get into the house.

Consult your doctor regarding the best way to handle an emergency situation like a flood or storm. Consider your strengths and questions you may consider. Stress is for instance one of the major causes in the situations mentioned above and it is possible to have a medical problem which stress can exacerbate. Blood pressure issues are one which is often brought to mind.

There have been limitations discussed in different aspects of the book. Medical issues constitute a major kind of restriction that should not be overlooked. Patients with high blood pressure as an example, might be advised against anything strenuous prior to, throughout or even following the storm.

Diabetics must ensure they are taking the right medications, as well as food options so they are able to eat regular meals without experiencing large fluctuations in blood sugar levels. Understanding the limitations of your have medical conditions and planning according to your needs.

If you are suffering from health issues, or have someone who has need to communicate contact details and plan a strategy to remain in contact throughout the weather. It is recommended to keep individuals around the person who has medical issues in the event that there is a problem. It is important to do this because it depends on the patient and the health issue concerned. There are some people who must keep a person with them however others may do easily by themselves. Give out telephone numbers, including home and cell numbers, and email addresses as well as Facebook and Twitter information. There are many methods to reach people we often come across alternative ways to contact them when phones are not working.

Three decades ago, when phones stopped working, it was impossible to connect with other individuals who weren't nearby. Nowadays, landline phones are only one method of reaching out to others. Create a list of telephone number, email address along with any other contact details. This will come in helpful for security and allows people to know that you're fine and not in need of help.

Following the hurricane, those with health issues or who are elderly could have trouble getting through their day to daily routine. One of the biggest challenges is cooking food. If there is no power or the cooking equipment, one might not be able cook healthy food.

It's good to know that most of the time, there are programs such as Meals on Wheels that come across and serve food to those who require these meals. You should keep their contact numbers handy.

It is also possible to prepare meals beforehand to feed the affected people through the most difficult portion of the storm, and afterward for a while. Cereals and other vegetables as well as bread and cold cuts will provide food even when there's nothing else.

## Chapter 12: Analysis

Tropical cyclones originate in tropical waters and derive their energy from warm waters. They start between 4deg 22deg S, and between the 4deg-35deg range of the equator.

The subtropical region of the northern hemisphere absorbs most of the power during the period of the summer (July-September). Massive circular (counterclockwise rotating) cells are formed in the process they can be categorized as hurricanes if they are located near North America or typhoons if they are formed in the west Pacific. The equatorial zones do have no tropical hurricanes. The time when the oceans are at their most hot, between May through November, over two-thirds of tropical storms occur throughout the north hemisphere with the highest intensity occurring in September and August.

The southern part of the hemisphere which is where they are often known by their name, cyclones. the peak occurs between the months of December through April, with their peak between winter months between January and February. While most people associate tropical cyclones to the damage they can cause through contact with the land, they are most part of the time of their "life" in the ocean and can be understood best as a result of the transfer of heat between the ocean and the atmosphere.

Moving heat energies from the ocean into the atmosphere is crucial to the formation of tropical cyclones. Low-pressure cell formation occurs near the surface of Earth and cause massive storms, as huge amounts of water-vaporized heated vapors move up.

The water vapor that's evaporated in the atmosphere will condense and cool during the process. At the end of the day it is possible to form storm clouds by this method. Large-scale convective clouds are created as the water begins returning towards the surface. During this process, the air mass is then compelled to spin because from the Coriolis Effect. Air masses move to the right side within the Northern hemisphere, and to towards the left within the southern part of the. The upward movement of warm water vapour has to be constantly replenished during storms to sustain themselves, otherwise, the storm will become worse before dissolving.

From storm to storm the various phases of creation differ significantly. The wind patterns that surround the center of the storm intensify when the pressure of the central region diminishes. The clouds begin to form in thin, swirling bands. The zone with the least pressure is called the storm's eye or central. The eye is not very active however the wall at the outer edge of the eye has the most powerful wind gusts as well as some of the most violent storms. 300 kilometers (186 miles) of winds that are hurricane force could exist outside of the eye. If a storm is traveling towards the north, it has the highest wind speeds in the northeastern quadrant due to the fact that the highest winds tend to occur just to the right of the center of the storm's direction.

Surface winds direct hurricane motion. Atlantic storms traverse in the Atlantic Ocean in a westward or northwesterly direction prior to making an abrupt turn towards the north before heading to north. The Coriolis phenomenon, caused due to the Earth's rotating, affects the curvature. Northern Pacific region is also a good example of this pattern. Although these patterns may be predetermined, every storm takes an individual course, and there are a variety of variations due to the conditions of the atmosphere near to the storm which act as steering force.

Storms generally travel across high-pressure and low-pressure systems. Wind movement being an effect of atmospheric pressure.

The animation below demonstrates how history tracks form patterns which demonstrate the way storms typically adhere to the same set of rules. This helps in mathematical modeling as well as projections of satellite data on the storm's routes. Temperatures of the ocean's surface are reduced due to the storm's interaction with the sea's surface. When the storm moves closer to the shoreline, it makes contact with the water in shallower depths and then begins to become involved with coastal structures.

Friction and the depletion of heat of the ocean "fuel" deplete the system's energy. This will then disappear once it is on land. The resulting storm surge occurs as a result of the storm that is in the ocean, can pose an extremely risk for those living near the shoreline close to the point that the ocean meets surface.

History

A few of the most famous hurricanes of U.S. history

1900 Galveston Hurricane

The 27th of August in The tropical Atlantic region witnessed the first sign of this dangerous storm system. It was a Category 4 hurricane at the time it struck land at the end of September 8, along the Texas coast to the south of Galveston. The storm swung north through the Great Plains after making landfall. In September 11, the storm changed its tropical features and began to shift towards its north-east eastern direction, spanning southern Canada, the Great Lakes, New England as well as southern Canada. It was one of the largest natural catastrophe of American time since it last was recorded on September 15.

Storm tides ranging from 8-15 feet were prevalent across Galveston Island as well as different areas along the Texas coast. According to reports, the storm could cause between 6,000 and 12,000 deaths, the majority that were caused by tide-related. The estimate of damages to property was around $30 million.

1928 San Felipe-Okeechobee Hurricane

While it is likely to have originated just a few days prior this common Cape Verde storm was first noticed in its tropical Atlantic on the 10th of September. On September 12 day, it passed by it the

Leeward Islands as it headed towards the west. The 13th (the San Felipe feast San Felipe) It hit directly on Puerto Rico as a Category 4 storm, before turning to the north-west and west.

After traversing the Bahamas as well as continuing to the west and northwestern, the storm struck Florida on the 16th of September close to Palm Beach. It was on the 17th when it moved to the north and northeast over to the Florida Peninsula, and on 19th September, its remnants reached east North Carolina. In September 20, the storm was heading north and joined with another non-tropical low in the east of Great Lakes. There are no reliable wind gauges accessible from the Florida area of landfall. The fourth strongest storm ever to arrive within the United States, according to Palm Beach, with a minimum pressure of 27.43 inches. San Juan, Puerto Rico has sustained speeds of 144 mph and Guayama recorded an 27.65-inch tension reading.

On its way across the Leeward Islands and eventually Florida the storm has caused many deaths as well as significant destruction to properties. The most significant disaster occurred at the inland portion of Florida's Lake Okeechobee when the storm resulted in a flood of the lake that ranged from 6 to 9 feet. Florida suffered 1,836 deaths predominantly due to the surge of the lake. Additionally, 312 additional persons died on the island of Puerto Rico, and 18 additional people are thought to have been killed on the Bahamas. Losses to property to Puerto Rico and Florida were valued at $25 million.

**Chapter 13: 1992 Hurricane Andrew**

On the 14th of August an unimportant tropical storm that came in the western part of Africa led to one of the deadliest storms that have struck this area of the United States.

On the 16th of August this wave was born into a tropical depression that the next day grew to become Tropical Storm Andrew. The advancing west-northwesterly Andrew was unable to overcome an upper-level trough that reduced the growth. Because of vertical wind shear in August 20 the storm essentially vanished. In the 21st of August Andrew was turning westward to an environment that seemed more comfortable and was half way across Bermuda as well as Puerto Rico.

Andrew rapidly increased its the strength to become an hurricane on the 22nd, and an Category 4 hurricane on the 23rd. The

24th of August Andrew returned to Category 4 in South Florida after temporarily losing it in the Bahamas.

The hurricane continued moving to the west, until it entered it into Gulf of Mexico, where it began moving to the to the north. The 26th of August Andrew was a Category 3 hurricane, struck land in the middle of the Louisiana coast because of this movement. The 28th of August was when Andrew was a part of an enveloping system following its turn toward the northeast. Based on information from barometers of private parties Andrew's center pressure at the landfall at Homestead, Florida, was 27.23 inches. That makes it the third most intense storm ever to strike this area of the United States.

The damages to the monitoring equipment kept the direct observation of Andrew's highest winds across South Florida. Fowey

Rocks' automated station registered sustained winds of 142 mph and speeds as high as the speed of 169 mph (measured by 144 feet up in the air) and higher readings could have been taken when the station was demolished and stopped recording. The peak speed recorded by the National Hurricane Center was 164 miles per hour, and an individual residence reported the speed as 171 miles per hour. Andrew caused a 17-foot hurricane surge that surrounded the Florida landing site, and storm tides that were around 8 feet swamped areas of the Louisiana shoreline.

Andrew brought 23 deaths within the United States and three more in the Bahamas. Andrew also caused a fatal twister in the southeast of Louisiana. Within the United States, the storm resulted in $26.5 billion of damage including $1 billion. was incurred in Louisiana as well as the remaining of the damage was in South Florida. The hurricanes that swept through Florida are the main cause for the devastation. Photos of Andrew can be found via the NASA Goddard Laboratory website. The Bahamas were hit by damage that was worth 250 million dollars.

2005 Hurricane Katrina

A single of the more devastating hurricanes to strike in American past history was Katrina. The storm struck Palm Beach-Lake Okeechobee, in the month of September 1928, it's turned into the biggest hurricane ever to strike in the United States.

The largest U.S. disaster ever, it caused devastating damage that was that was estimated to be $75 billion the New Orleans region and down the Mississippi coast. S. largest hurricane ever. A tropical wave and an upper-level trough as well as the remnants from Tropical Depression Ten came together in the creation of this catastrophic tropical storm. On the 23rd of August the tropical depression formed about 200 miles to the southeast from Nassau, Bahamas.

It then moved northwards over the following day, and eventually reaching 75 miles east-southeast from Nassau in the form of tropical Storm Katrina. Between August 24 and 25 The storm moved through Northwest Bahamas before turning to the west, headed towards the southern part of Florida.

The 26th of August the storm travelled across the southern part of Florida before reaching Eastern Gulf of Mexico from the southwest. Following that, Katrina became substantially stronger and intensified to a the category 5 level on August 28. On the same day, there was an intense storm that was of 195 miles to the southeast of entrance to the Mississippi River with maximum sustained winds of 175mph, and an average pressure of 902 millibars as recorded by an aircraft.

At a maximum speed of around 125 miles per hour (Category 3) Katrina's central region reached land near Buras, Louisiana around 1110 UTC on the 29th of August as it turned towards the northwest, then to the north.

Although Katrina diminished as it moved across the land towards the north-northeast but it was still an active hurricane as it sped towards Laurel, Mississippi. The 30th of August the storm weakened and turned into an tropical depression in the Tennessee Valley. The 31st of August Katrina transformed into an extratropical low and on the same day, across Eastern Great Lakes, a frontal zone was able to absorb it. Southeast Louisiana, southern Mississippi and the southwest region of Alabama all saw hurricane-like weather conditions due to Katrina.

On August 29, Grand Isle, Louisiana, Coastal Marine Automated Network (C-MAN) station reported the average speed of winds for 10 minutes at 85 mph, with a maximum of at 114 speeds. With the number of stations affected, power cut off, or had their communications cut off due to the storm, greater speeds are likely to have occurred there as well as elsewhere. Some parts along the Mississippi coast saw floods from storm surges that ranged from up to 25-28 feet above normal tide levels. Likewise, the Southern Louisiana coast saw storm surge flooding that was up to 20-feet above normal levels of tide. Furthermore The Dry Tortugas and southern Florida witnessed hurricane-like conditions.

As of 01:15 UTC, August 26th, at 01:15 UTC on August 26, National Hurricane

Center recorded steady temperatures of 69mph and speeds of 87 mph. Also, tropical storm-like conditions prevailed within areas like the Florida Keys and throughout the northern Gulf coast to as to the easternmost part in the west Florida Panhandle. Eight to twelve inches of rainfall fell on Katrina's route inland away from northern Gulf coast. In contrast, 10-14 inches fell over the southern part of Florida. The tornadoes produced by the storm were 33 as per accounts. There were 1200 reported deaths as a result of Katrina which included around 1000 of them occurring in Louisiana as well as 200 deaths in Mississippi.

Southern Florida saw the fatalities of seven more people. Southern Mississippi and southeast Louisiana were devastated in the wake of Katrina.

A number of structures in the Mississippi coast were ruined due to the surge of storms, and also wrought damage miles to the inland. The southeast from New Orleans, in parts of the southeast region of Louisiana the area was also devastated by similar damage. Within New Orleans, in the New Orleans metropolitan region, the storm surge pushed over and ruptured levees and flooded the entirety of the city's east suburbs. Katrina's winds ravaged in the inland region, reaching north Mississippi as well as Alabama. In Miami-Dade as well as Broward counties hurricane also caused flooding and wind damage.

1893 Hurricane Cheniere Caminada

A storm that hit the the barrier islands of South Louisiana near the entry point to Barataria Bay on October 2 in 1893. The storm struck Cheniere Caminada directly, flooding the community of fishermen with a 16-foot storm surge which killed animals, people crop, property, and livestock almost completely removing it out of existence. Based on current estimations it is believed that it was Cheniere Caminada storm was a category 4 hurricane at the time it struck land and killed more than 2,000 residents within the region and ranked as one of the most destructive storms that have struck Louisiana.

From Louisiana from Louisiana to Bay St. Louis, Mississippi from Bay St. Louis to Mississippi, Louisiana and Mobile, Alabama, the destruction caused by the storm was extensive.

But, as Cheniere Caminada inhabitants were the most impacted by the storm They weighed their loss and attempted to rebuild. A few people from the community who lived there before the disaster are still in place today, as many of its inhabitants moved away within the next couple of years. It is now referred to by the name of Cheniere Caminada Hurricane of 1893 due to its ties to the fishing community, as well as its tragic story.

Cheniere Caminada was nearly erased from the maps, however three of her literary masterpieces are able to preserve the history of the storm that struck 1893. Kate Chopin, a writer who was from Louisiana who often was a summer visitor to close by Grand Isle, wrote the three works right after the storm.

After the storm, Chopin created her short story "At Cheniere Caminada" when she was informed of the efforts undertaken to save and help locals. Chopin's most famous work, The Awakening, a publication that was written a year before the hurricane struck Grand Isle, poignantly praises Cheniere Caminada's residents and the communities prior to the disaster. Chopin uses allusions to the impact of the hurricane to Cheniere Caminada and its residents in both works, in the form of a reference or indirect.

Falls' Cheniere Caminada, Or the Wind of Death, which comprises stories of Cheniere Caminada locals on their experiences with the hurricane. It is an end-of-the-line work which was made available the year as the catastrophe. Falls examines the story of the storm as being one of the most destructive hurricanes as well as the forced eviction Cheniere locals of the city faced as they evaluate the impact of the storm.

The 4th of October 1886 hurricane that hit Johnson's Bayou and Sabine Pass that killed 50 persons and numerous cattle, as well as the Last Island Hurricane of August 1856, that claimed over 200 lives on the famous island resort, were the only two storms to resemble that of the Cheniere Caminada Hurricane of 1893. None of them came close to that of more than 2

000 deaths after that storm, for which Cheniere Caminada was named.

## Chapter 14: Safety & Survival

What is one to do in the case of a storm? What should you do in the lead-up to, during, and following a storm. It's essential that you be prepared if you live in an area where you are vulnerable.

In the days before the hurricane

Secure your valuables. The best window security for doors and windows comes from permanently installed storm shutters. Another alternative is to put up boards the windows with five-inch" marine plywood which has been cut into dimensions and ready to install. Windows' glass can crack even with tape. If you want to secure your roof to frame's structure, make use of straps or additional clips. It will limit damages to your roof. You can reduce the risk of breaking branches and other debris by trimming plants and trees around the house.

In order to avoid flooding that is not intended Clean up loose and blockages in drains and gutters. Choose where and how you will protect your boat, if you own one.

Make sure that your items are elevated within your basement in order to stop any minor flooding from destroying these items. Set any important items on top shelves or on a different level within your house. Photograph albums and other items fall into the category of. Make sure you have tight-fitting lids for the home chemical products and keep them in high-end shelves. Floods and chemicals can be very dangerous and fatal.

Make a plan to build a safe area. Invest in a fire extinguisher. Make sure that your pets are identified. Make a list of all the documents that you can bring along to use the documents for an insurance.

Photograph or scan vital documents such as prescriptions, passports, social security cards, drivers' licenses and other official documents. For the photos to be saved and upload them to the internet, you can do so. Make copies of them inside a bag which is water-proof. If power goes out make sure you have an emergency kit. Included are prescribed medications, as well as three days worth of water, food and cash (along with any pets).

Make time to look around and find all refuges within your area. Keep an eye on the escape route. If needed, carry an "to go" bag on the go.

Put water in plastic bottles to drink. Think about what you'd need should a power cut force you to live for several days on your own. Make sure you have enough fuel in your automobiles. Download your Red Cross Emergency App on your Android or iPhone. Also, you can send the text "GETCANE" to 90999.

As a Hurricane Draws Near

What you need to do during the case of an occurrence of

Stay up-to-date on the weather's updates via local radio stations, NOAA television, radio and on the web to remain up-to-date. Make sure you are aware of any evacuation announcements.

Shut down the storm shutters, and make sure your home is secured. The force of strong winds can be enough to raise and even break Awnings that could turn into projectiles. Take inside or secure all outdoor furniture, barbecues, trash cans, bicycles hanging plants, toys and garden equipment.

If you are told by authorities to shut off the appliances. If not, adjust the temperature of the refrigerator as well as freezer to the coldest setting and ensure that the doors shut. Remove freezer-friendly items from the fridge. OFFSET those propane tanks.

In order to avoid water damage In order to avoid damage from water, move any devices onto higher shelves. In order to ensure it's ready to go, ensure that your cell phone recharged. After that, do not make use of the phone unless you are in an situation that requires it. Remember that you have to keep the required amount in your bank. An interruption in electricity could hinder ATMs' operation. If you're in the mood take the time to put your boat in a mooring. You should ensure that there is enough water for hygiene purposes for cleaning or flushing toilets.

Put water in the tub or other containers that are large.

Make sure you have the following things such as a fire extinguisher emergency first aid kit Kit for medications prescribed by a doctor with batteries and flashlights blankets and sleeping bags food and cooking utensils containers for water bottles, canned food items as well as jumper cables. Paper maps and GPS, GPS toilet paper, additional personal items for care as well as rain equipment. Keep your home safe.

If there's a mandate by your local authority to evacuate, follow the instructions and implement them immediately. Whatever way they're anchored in the soil, storms can cause serious danger for those who live in a mobile house or similar temporary structures. The risk of hurricanes is greater when you are at higher elevations. So be cautious if you live in a building that is high-rise.

If your house is located situated near to an inland canal, river, seashore, floodplain or and you're worried your security could be in the risk, it's advisable to plan for an evacuation

In the event that you split up set up a place to meet to bring your family together. Uncertainty about whether loved ones are protected in a hurricane is among the most significant issues with these kinds of situations. Be aware that there are times when mobile phones aren't functioning. Communication prior to the phone is essential. When the authorities are satisfied that it safe, do not go back. Avoid any water that has risen. Do not travel on roads that have been flooded on foot or in a car.

In the event of a hurricane

Make sure you are in your safe space in case you haven't yet made the move. If you do not have any safe place, be sure to adhere to these guidelines:

Don't go near the glass doors and windows, as well as ensure that you remain in the interior of your home. Secure and brace the exterior doors and close all the internal doors. Close the curtains and blinds shut. If the weather is calm don't be fooled as it could be a sign of the eye of the storm, and then the wind will pick again. Find safety in an interior space, like a closet or the lower level of a hallway. Place yourself on the floor beneath the table or another substantial object.

Following the storm

The process of recovering from an accident is often a lengthy process. It is the most important thing to consider safety and physical and mental well-being. Family members should be advised that you're safe and out from danger. In order to avoid electrical dangers and other risks, you shouldn't leave home until after you're allowed to. In the event that you are not allowed to do so, don't drinking water from the tap. Check the refrigerator or freezer's temperature. It is safe to consume food which has been kept below 40°F or lower. If it is not, throw it away in order to avoid harm.

Get rid of all food items that comes in contact the floodwaters also, as it could contain chemical and water-borne illness, among others. It is better to be safe rather than regretting. Call your insurance company and document the damage.

Dry or remove water damaged items from your home immediately. It is crucial to limit the likelihood of mold developing inside your house. Avoid dangerously charged, contaminated and electrically charged flooding. A mere six inches of floodwater could throw a mature man to the floor. Don't underestimate the power of water that is flowing.

## Chapter 15: Understanding The Formation And Basics Of Hurricanes

The term "hurricane" is also used to refer to storms, cyclones or typhoons based upon the area they are among nature's most devastating and powerful force. The massive storms are distinguished by high storms, heavy rain, as well as a distinctive circular movement.

A hurricane is an enormous tropical storm that develops in warm ocean waters close to the ocean's equator. The energy source is the warmth contained in the ocean's warm surface.

The main distinguishing characteristic of an eye in a hurricane is the tranquil, circular space in its center. It is then with a backdrop of high-flying clouds as well as intense wind gusts.

1. The Components: Warm Ocean Waters and Moisture

The development of a storm needs specific oceanic and atmospheric conditions. Ocean waters that are warm, and with temperatures that are at or below 26.5 degree Celsius (80 Celsius) provide the catalyst for these storms.

The hot water evaporates, forming humid air which rises, and creates clouds. The process then lets heat out into the atmosphere which further heats the air around it.

2. The Birth of a Hurricane: The Coriolis Effect

In order for a storm to develop it is necessary that the Coriolis effect resulting from the Earth's rotating function. The Coriolis influence causes the air to revolve around a low pressure center in a counterclockwise direction within the Northern Hemisphere and a clockwise direction within the Southern Hemisphere. This is vital for the beginning of a storm.

3. Formation of a Tropical Disturbance:

The sequence begins by forming the tropical disturbance, which is a collection of storms that rage over warmer ocean water. When the humid, warm air increases, it gets cooler as water vapour evaporates, which releases latent heat.

This release of heat warms surrounding air and causes it to rise too. The upward motion of moist, warm air causes a zone that is low in pressure near the top of the mountain.

4. The Tropical Depression Stage:

If the climate remains positive and the disturbance increases in the strength it could transform into the form of a tropical depression. At this point, the low pressure system begins to move, propelled by the

Coriolis effects. When the air is soaring towards the middle the system, it draws additional moisture at the ocean's surface and fuels the growth of the storm.

5. From Depression to Storm: Tropical Storm Formation

The sustained winds in the middle of the depression exceed a certain level (usually 39 miles per hour or 63 kilometers/h) The system gets transformed into the status of a tropical storm.

In this stage, the storm has an official title. The warm waters of the ocean remain to supply power to the storm which allows it to get stronger.

6. Formation of a Full Hurricane:

As the tropical storm builds greater energy and water and moisture, it may transform into an actual hurricane. In this phase, the central region of the storm, known as the eye, forms. The eye is a tranquil region, that is characterized by blue skies.

The warm air that is escaping from on the surface of the sea rises up in the center of the ocean, forming an area of low pressure that draws air from the nearby zone.

7. The Eye Wall and Intense Winds:

Around the eye is the eye wall, a zone of violent thunderstorms, with the most powerful winds during hurricanes. The atmosphere in the eye wall is drawn down from the upper levels of the atmosphere and helps clear the skies, and establish the peaceful central area. But, the air that is descending produces a wall of powerful wind that slant upward outward.

8. Lifecycle and Dissipation:

When a storm moves across more chilly waters, or comes into contact with the land surface, it is unable to access the source of warm, humid air. Consequently, its energy source diminishes.

In the absence of warmer water to fuel the storm, the storm becomes weaker, and it eventually dies.

Yet, hurricanes are able to cause heavy rain, powerful storms, and even flooding when they are weaker.

Hurricane Categories

Hurricanes are classified based upon their sustained winds by using the scale Saffir-Simpson. The scale spans between category 1 (weakest) up to Cat five (strongest). Category 5 hurricanes sustain wind speeds that exceed 157 mph (252 kilometers/h) and could cause devastating damages.

The Saffir-Simpson Hurricane Wind Scale is important tool in assessing and classifying the strength of hurricanes.

In the beginning of the 1970s, it was created by engineers Herbert Saffir and meteorologist Robert Simpson The scale helped emergency personnel, meteorologists as well as the general public to understand the impact of a hurricane that is about to hit.

The classification of hurricanes is based on five categories, based on the sustained winds they sustain, with each category having its own distinctive characteristics and risks.

Category 1. Minimal Hurricane (74-95 mph)

Category 1 hurricanes can be most gentle on the scale of Saffir-Simpson. Though they're relatively light speed of winds compared to the more affluent categories, they may nevertheless cause harm. Be prepared for winds of between 74 and 95 miles/hour (119 to 153 kilometres per hour) during an Category 1 hurricane.

They can also rip up tiny trees, power lines and other outdoors objects that aren't secured. It is possible to have roof and siding damages, but houses that are constructed well will generally survive.

Cat 2: Medium Storm (96-110 miles per hour)

Category 2 hurricanes are greater winds than Category I storms. They have sustained speeds of 100 to 96 miles/hour (154 to 177 km each hour).

As the level increases, the risk of damage is significantly increased. Windows, roofs, as well as doors could suffer significant destruction, while trees may be snared or uprooted. The power outages are frequent however, some regions may suffer flooding as a result of the heavy rain.

Category 3: Large-scale hurricane (111-129 miles per hour)

An Category 3 storm can be considered to be a major storm. Its winds range from between 111 and 129 miles per hour (178 to 208 km per hour) It can create massive destruction. Buildings and homes could lose the roof, while smaller structures may be completely destroyed.

The increase in storm surge is a major concern, leading to flooding of the coastal areas. The evacuation orders are usually given to areas that are that are in the direction of the category 3 hurricane.

Cat 4: Extreme Hurricane (130-156 mph)

Cat 4 hurricanes are extraordinarily intense, sustaining speed of winds that range from 130-156 miles an hour (209 to

251 km each hour). The storms could cause severe damages, which can include the destruction of walls and roofing within well-constructed homes.

A lot of power poles and trees fall, which causes long power outages. The areas along the coast are susceptible from severe storm surges as well as inland flooding is the biggest danger.

Categor 5. Catastrophic Hurricane (157 mph or greater)

Cat 5 hurricanes are the most destructive and powerful storms in the Saffir-Simpson scale. They can sustain sustained winds that are 157 miles per hour (252 kilometers per hour) or more.

www.ingramcontent.com/pod-product-compliance
Lightning Source LLC
Chambersburg PA
CBHW070555010526
44118CB00012B/1329